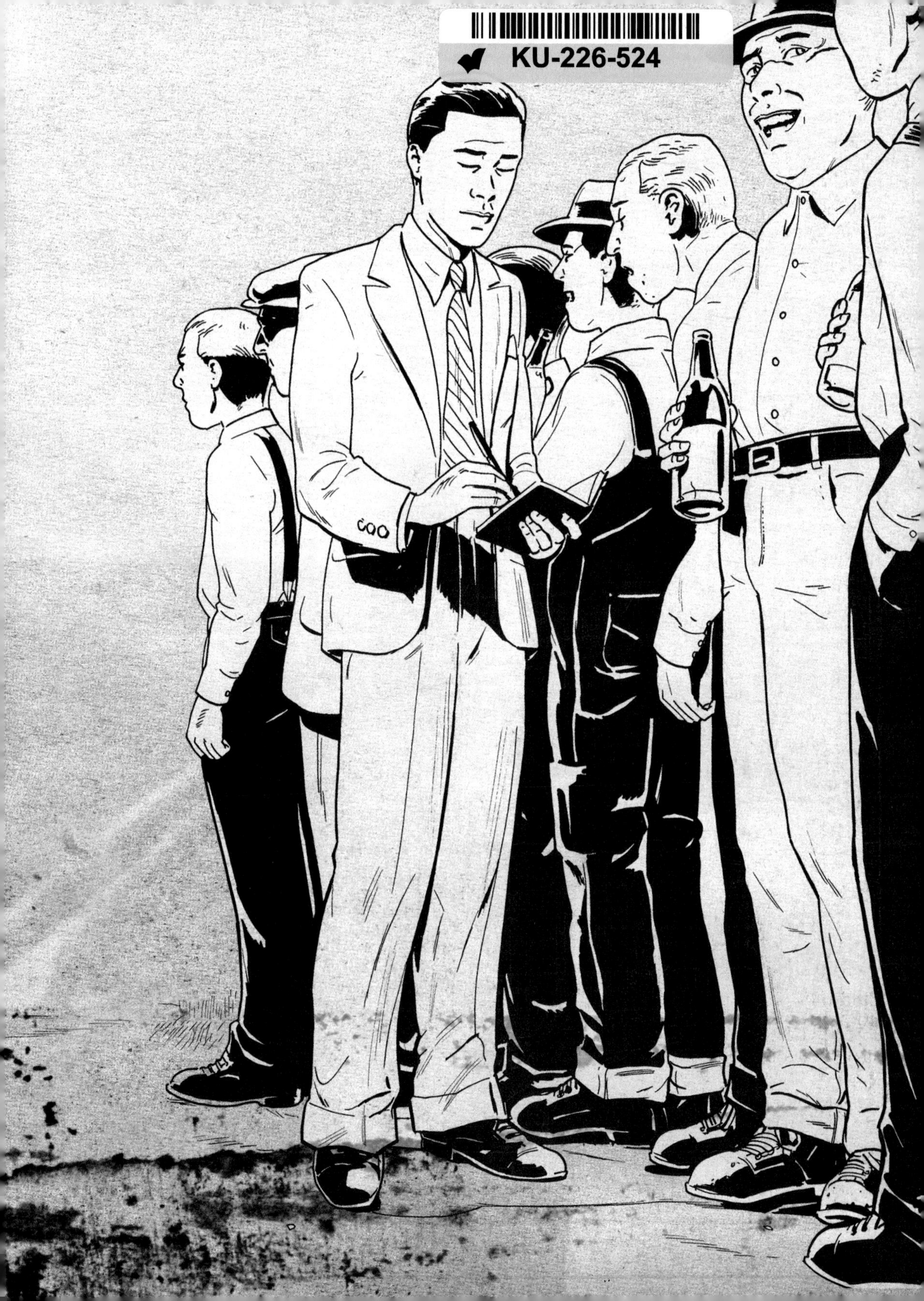

Author's Note

I grew up a black boy who looked white. This was in a predominantly African-American neighborhood, during the height of the Black Power era, so I stood out a bit. My mom even got me a dashiki so I could fit in with the other kids, but the contrast between the colorful African garb and my nearly blond, straight brown hair just made things worse. Along with my cousin (half black/half Jewish) I started fantasizing about living in another time, another situation, where my ethnic appearance would be an asset instead of a burden. We would "go Incognegro," we told ourselves as we ran around, pretending to be race spies in the war against white supremacy.

I forgot my "Incognegro" dreams until college, when I read about Walter White, the former head of the NAACP. White was an African-American even paler than I was. In the early 20th century, White went undercover, posing as a white man in the deep south to investigate lynchings. It was as if my little childhood fantasy had come to life. From then on, the idea continued to gestate. I started feeling that what once seemed silly was turning into something I had to write about.

The birth of my twins in 2005, one of whom is brown-skinned with black Afro hair, the other with the palest of pink skins and more European curly hair, brought the rest of the story home to me. Two people with the exact same ethnic lineage destined to be viewed differently only because of genetic randomness. From there, the story found itself.

And now it finds you.

— **Mat Johnson**

Karen Berger Sr. VP-Executive Editor   **Jonathan Vankin** Editor   **Mark Doyle** Assistant Editor   **Louis Prandi** Art Director
Paul Levitz President & Publisher   **Georg Brewer** VP-Design & DC Direct Creative   **Richard Bruning** Sr. VP-Creative Director
Patrick Caldon Exec. VP-Finance & Operations   **Chris Caramalis** VP-Finance   **John Cunningham** VP-Marketing
Terri Cunningham VP-Managing Editor   **Alison Gill** VP-Manufacturing   **David Hyde** VP-Publicity
Hank Kanalz VP-General Manager, WildStorm   **Jim Lee** Editorial Director-WildStorm   **Paula Lowitt** Sr. VP-Business & Legal Affairs
MaryEllen McLaughlin VP-Advertising & Custom Publishing   **John Nee** Sr. VP-Business Development
Gregory Noveck Sr. VP-Creative Affairs   **Sue Pohja** VP-Book Trade Sales   **Steve Rotterdam** Sr. VP-Sales & Marketing
Cheryl Rubin Sr. VP-Brand Management   **Jeff Trojan** VP-Business Development, DC Direct   **Bob Wayne** VP-Sales
Cover photograph by **Stephen John Phillips**

PART I

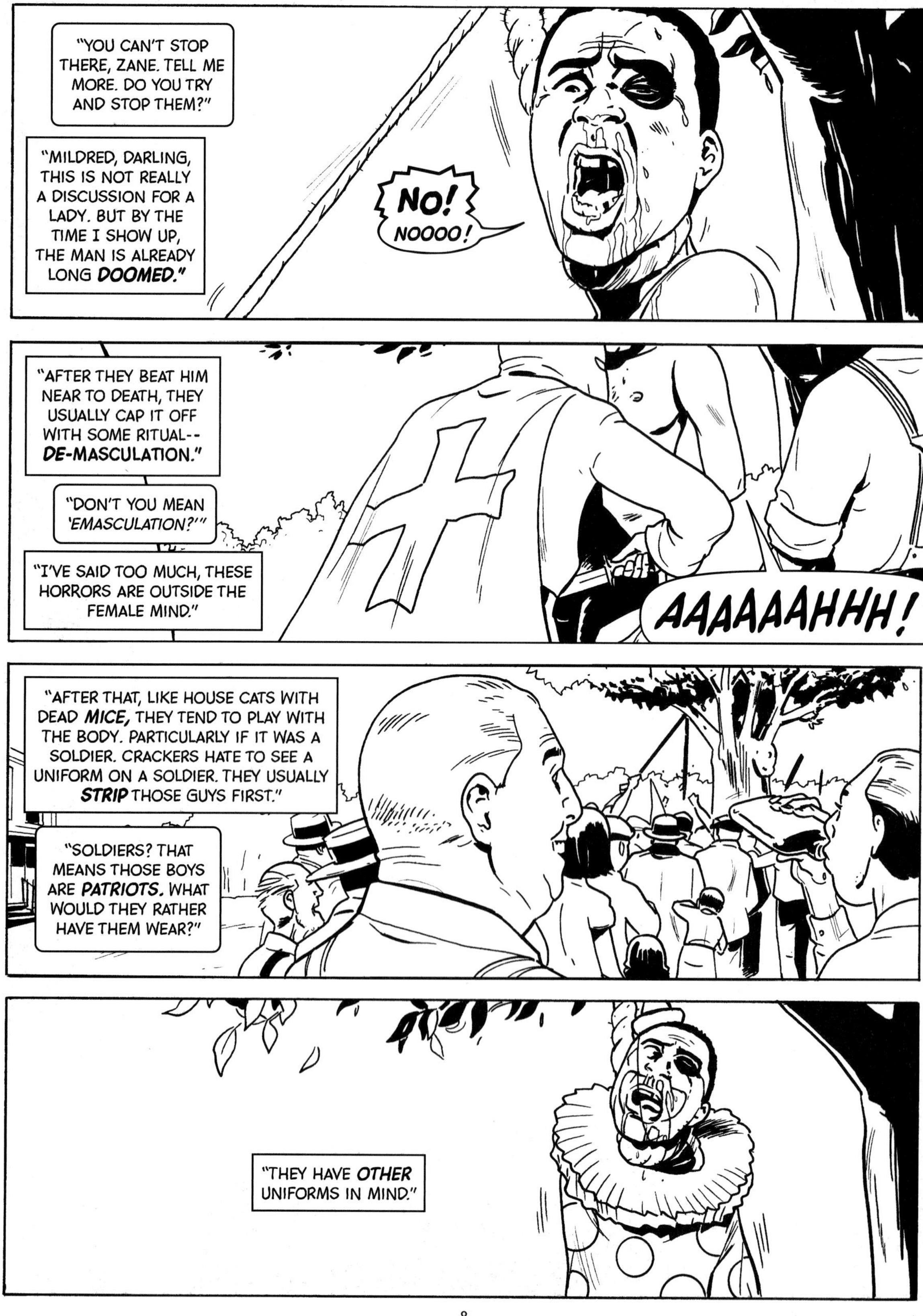
"YOU CAN'T STOP THERE, ZANE. TELL ME MORE. DO YOU TRY AND STOP THEM?"
"MILDRED, DARLING, THIS IS NOT REALLY A DISCUSSION FOR A LADY. BUT BY THE TIME I SHOW UP, THE MAN IS ALREADY LONG DOOMED."
NO! NOOOO!
"AFTER THEY BEAT HIM NEAR TO DEATH, THEY USUALLY CAP IT OFF WITH SOME RITUAL-- DE-MASCULATION."
"DON'T YOU MEAN 'EMASCULATION?'"
"I'VE SAID TOO MUCH, THESE HORRORS ARE OUTSIDE THE FEMALE MIND."
AAAAAAHHH!
"AFTER THAT, LIKE HOUSE CATS WITH DEAD MICE, THEY TEND TO PLAY WITH THE BODY. PARTICULARLY IF IT WAS A SOLDIER. CRACKERS HATE TO SEE A UNIFORM ON A SOLDIER. THEY USUALLY STRIP THOSE GUYS FIRST."
"SOLDIERS? THAT MEANS THOSE BOYS ARE PATRIOTS. WHAT WOULD THEY RATHER HAVE THEM WEAR?"
"THEY HAVE OTHER UNIFORMS IN MIND."

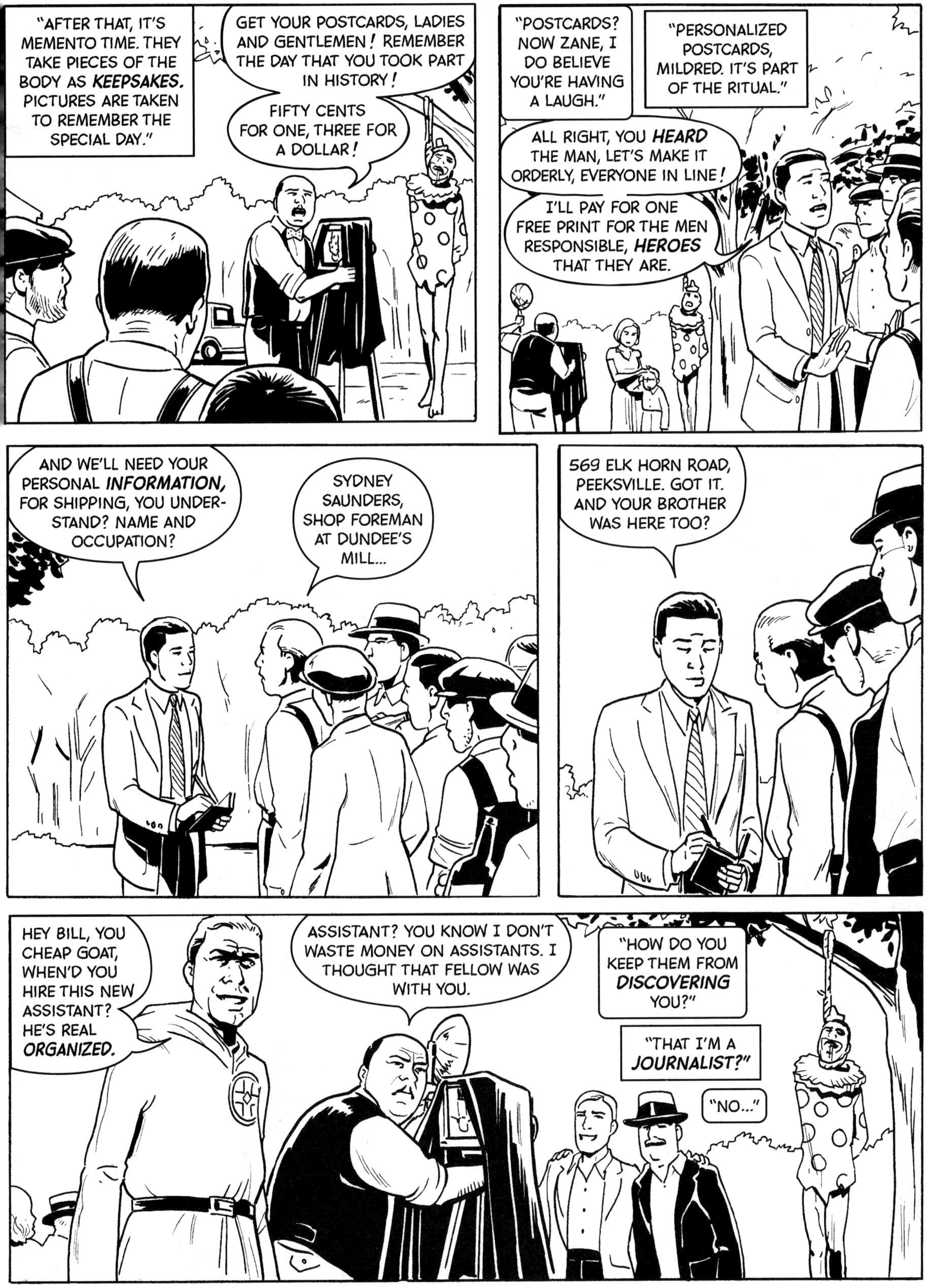
"AFTER THAT, IT'S MEMENTO TIME. THEY TAKE PIECES OF THE BODY AS KEEPSAKES. PICTURES ARE TAKEN TO REMEMBER THE SPECIAL DAY."
GET YOUR POSTCARDS, LADIES AND GENTLEMEN! REMEMBER THE DAY THAT YOU TOOK PART IN HISTORY!
FIFTY CENTS FOR ONE, THREE FOR A DOLLAR!
"POSTCARDS? NOW ZANE, I DO BELIEVE YOU'RE HAVING A LAUGH."
"PERSONALIZED POSTCARDS, MILDRED. IT'S PART OF THE RITUAL."
ALL RIGHT, YOU HEARD THE MAN, LET'S MAKE IT ORDERLY, EVERYONE IN LINE!
I'LL PAY FOR ONE FREE PRINT FOR THE MEN RESPONSIBLE, HEROES THAT THEY ARE.
AND WE'LL NEED YOUR PERSONAL INFORMATION, FOR SHIPPING, YOU UNDERSTAND? NAME AND OCCUPATION?
SYDNEY SAUNDERS, SHOP FOREMAN AT DUNDEE'S MILL...
569 ELK HORN ROAD, PEEKSVILLE. GOT IT. AND YOUR BROTHER WAS HERE TOO?
HEY BILL, YOU CHEAP GOAT, WHEN'D YOU HIRE THIS NEW ASSISTANT? HE'S REAL ORGANIZED.
ASSISTANT? YOU KNOW I DON'T WASTE MONEY ON ASSISTANTS. I THOUGHT THAT FELLOW WAS WITH YOU.
"HOW DO YOU KEEP THEM FROM DISCOVERING YOU?"
"THAT I'M A JOURNALIST?"
"NO..."

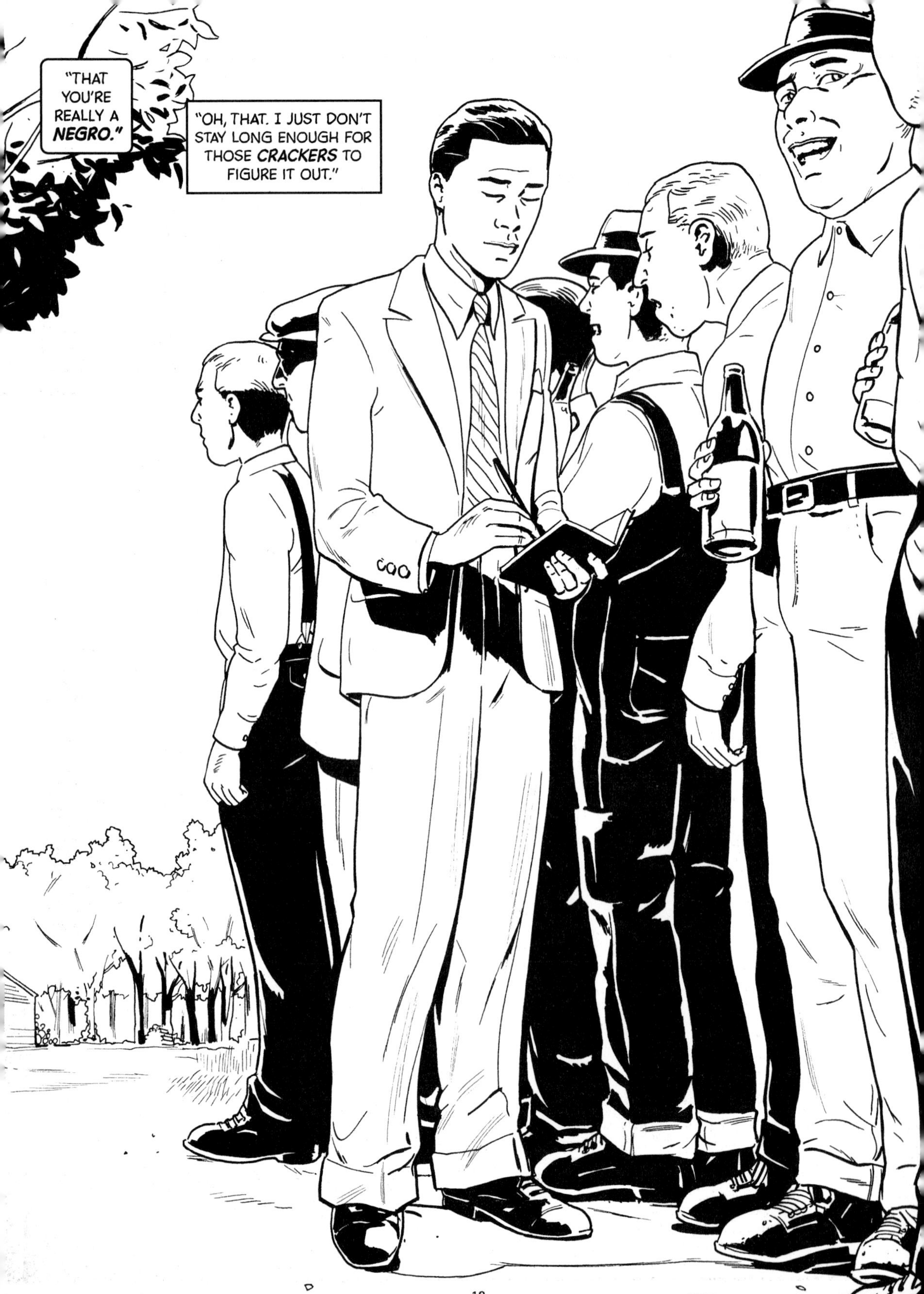
"THAT YOU'RE REALLY A **NEGRO.**"
"OH, THAT. I JUST DON'T STAY LONG ENOUGH FOR THOSE **CRACKERS** TO FIGURE IT OUT."

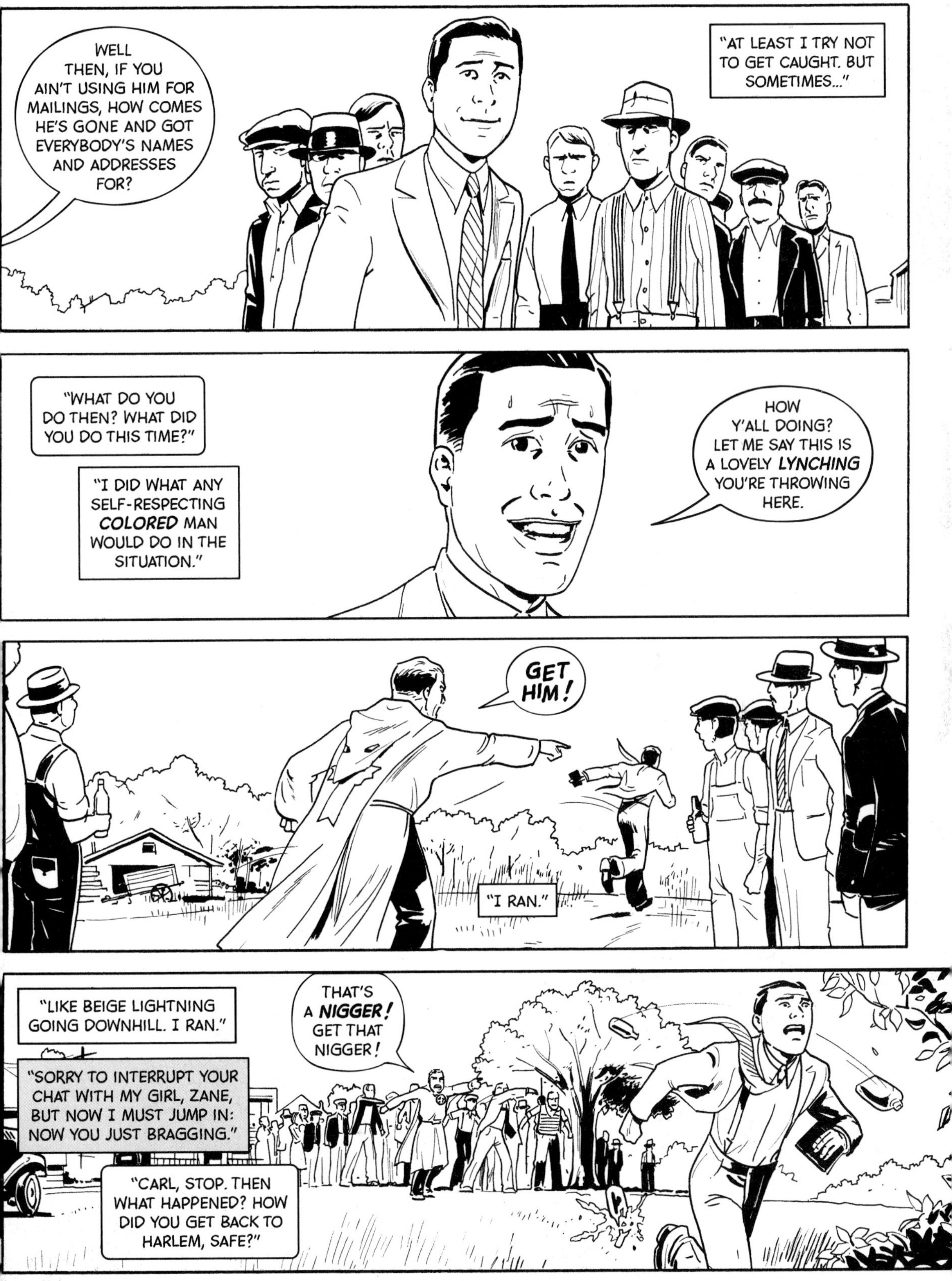
WELL THEN, IF YOU AIN'T USING HIM FOR MAILINGS, HOW COMES HE'S GONE AND GOT EVERYBODY'S NAMES AND ADDRESSES FOR?
"AT LEAST I TRY NOT TO GET CAUGHT. BUT SOMETIMES..."
"WHAT DO YOU DO THEN? WHAT DID YOU DO THIS TIME?"
"I DID WHAT ANY SELF-RESPECTING COLORED MAN WOULD DO IN THE SITUATION."
HOW Y'ALL DOING? LET ME SAY THIS IS A LOVELY LYNCHING YOU'RE THROWING HERE.
GET HIM!
"I RAN."
"LIKE BEIGE LIGHTNING GOING DOWNHILL. I RAN."
THAT'S A NIGGER! GET THAT NIGGER!
"SORRY TO INTERRUPT YOUR CHAT WITH MY GIRL, ZANE, BUT NOW I MUST JUMP IN: NOW YOU JUST BRAGGING."
"CARL, STOP. THEN WHAT HAPPENED? HOW DID YOU GET BACK TO HARLEM, SAFE?"

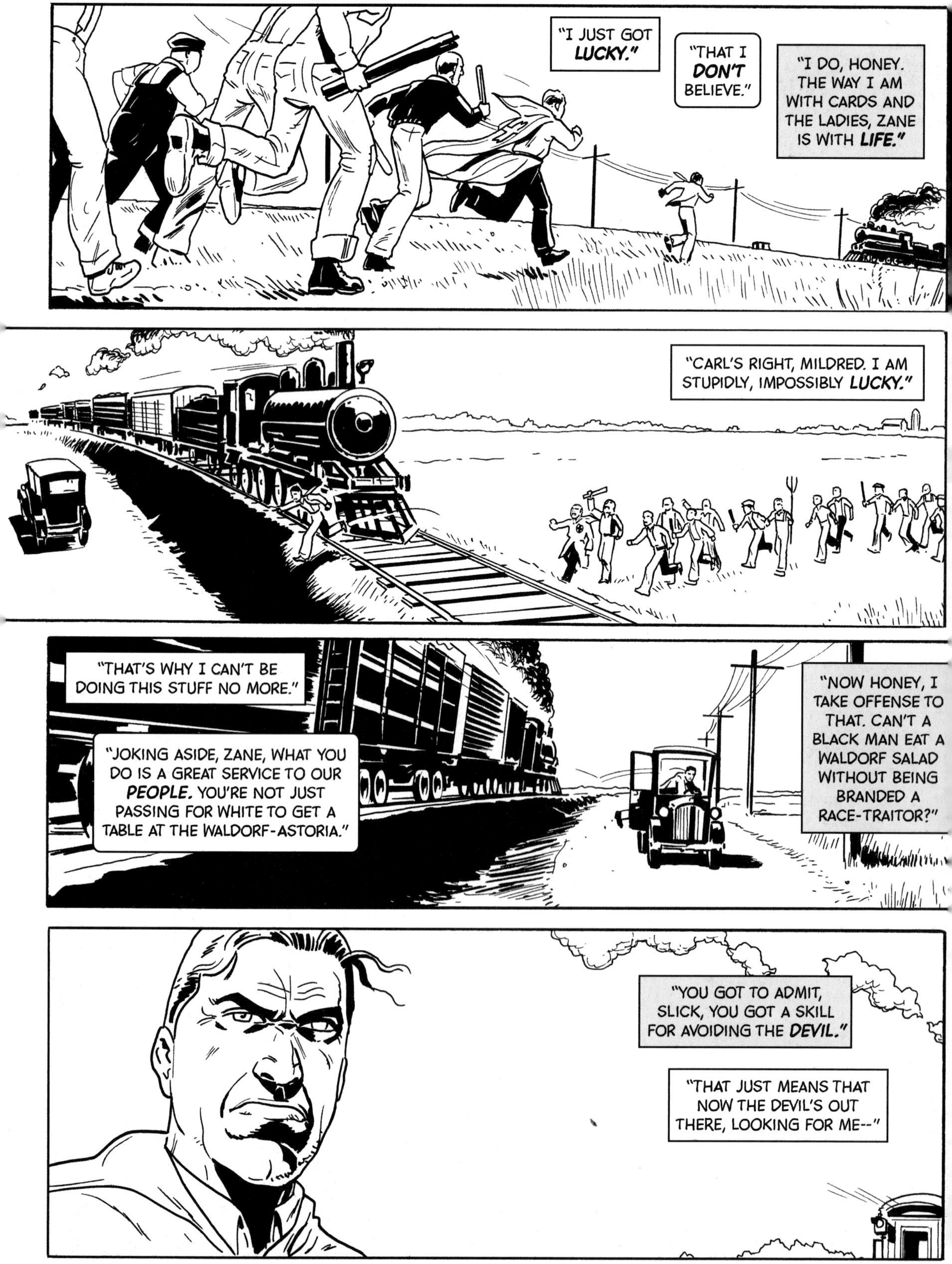
"I JUST GOT LUCKY."
"THAT I DON'T BELIEVE."
"I DO, HONEY. THE WAY I AM WITH CARDS AND THE LADIES, ZANE IS WITH LIFE."
"CARL'S RIGHT, MILDRED. I AM STUPIDLY, IMPOSSIBLY LUCKY."
"THAT'S WHY I CAN'T BE DOING THIS STUFF NO MORE."
"JOKING ASIDE, ZANE, WHAT YOU DO IS A GREAT SERVICE TO OUR PEOPLE. YOU'RE NOT JUST PASSING FOR WHITE TO GET A TABLE AT THE WALDORF-ASTORIA."
"NOW HONEY, I TAKE OFFENSE TO THAT. CAN'T A BLACK MAN EAT A WALDORF SALAD WITHOUT BEING BRANDED A RACE-TRAITOR?"
"YOU GOT TO ADMIT, SLICK, YOU GOT A SKILL FOR AVOIDING THE DEVIL."
"THAT JUST MEANS THAT NOW THE DEVIL'S OUT THERE, LOOKING FOR ME--"

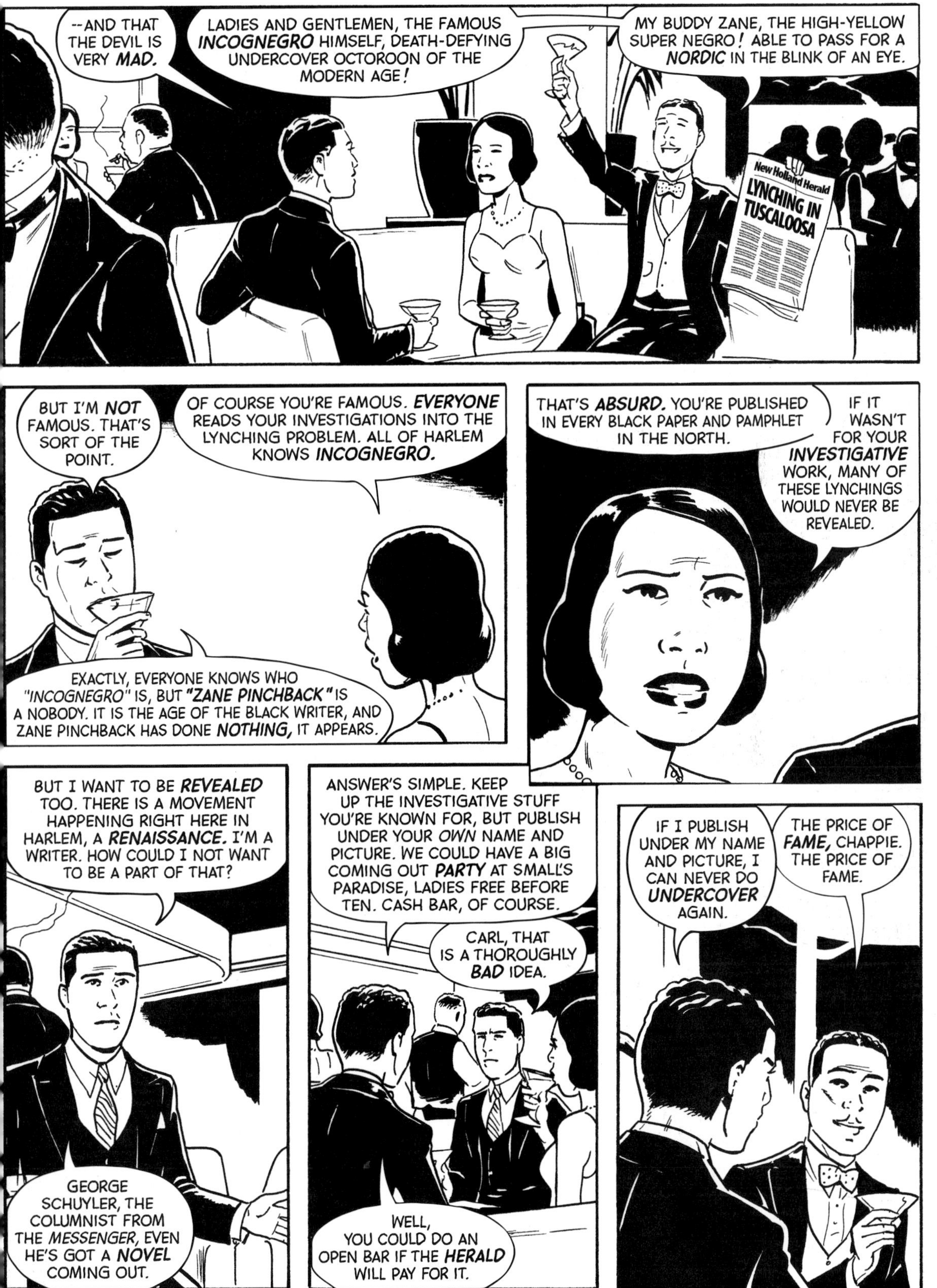
--AND THAT THE DEVIL IS VERY MAD.
LADIES AND GENTLEMEN, THE FAMOUS INCOGNEGRO HIMSELF, DEATH-DEFYING UNDERCOVER OCTOROON OF THE MODERN AGE!
MY BUDDY ZANE, THE HIGH-YELLOW SUPER NEGRO! ABLE TO PASS FOR A NORDIC IN THE BLINK OF AN EYE.
New Holland Herald
LYNCHING IN TUSCALOOSA
BUT I'M NOT FAMOUS. THAT'S SORT OF THE POINT.
OF COURSE YOU'RE FAMOUS. EVERYONE READS YOUR INVESTIGATIONS INTO THE LYNCHING PROBLEM. ALL OF HARLEM KNOWS INCOGNEGRO.
EXACTLY, EVERYONE KNOWS WHO "INCOGNEGRO" IS, BUT "ZANE PINCHBACK" IS A NOBODY. IT IS THE AGE OF THE BLACK WRITER, AND ZANE PINCHBACK HAS DONE NOTHING, IT APPEARS.
THAT'S ABSURD. YOU'RE PUBLISHED IN EVERY BLACK PAPER AND PAMPHLET IN THE NORTH.
IF IT WASN'T FOR YOUR INVESTIGATIVE WORK, MANY OF THESE LYNCHINGS WOULD NEVER BE REVEALED.
BUT I WANT TO BE REVEALED TOO. THERE IS A MOVEMENT HAPPENING RIGHT HERE IN HARLEM, A RENAISSANCE. I'M A WRITER. HOW COULD I NOT WANT TO BE A PART OF THAT?
GEORGE SCHUYLER, THE COLUMNIST FROM THE MESSENGER, EVEN HE'S GOT A NOVEL COMING OUT.
ANSWER'S SIMPLE. KEEP UP THE INVESTIGATIVE STUFF YOU'RE KNOWN FOR, BUT PUBLISH UNDER YOUR OWN NAME AND PICTURE. WE COULD HAVE A BIG COMING OUT PARTY AT SMALL'S PARADISE, LADIES FREE BEFORE TEN. CASH BAR, OF COURSE.
CARL, THAT IS A THOROUGHLY BAD IDEA.
WELL, YOU COULD DO AN OPEN BAR IF THE HERALD WILL PAY FOR IT.
IF I PUBLISH UNDER MY NAME AND PICTURE, I CAN NEVER DO UNDERCOVER AGAIN.
THE PRICE OF FAME, CHAPPIE. THE PRICE OF FAME.

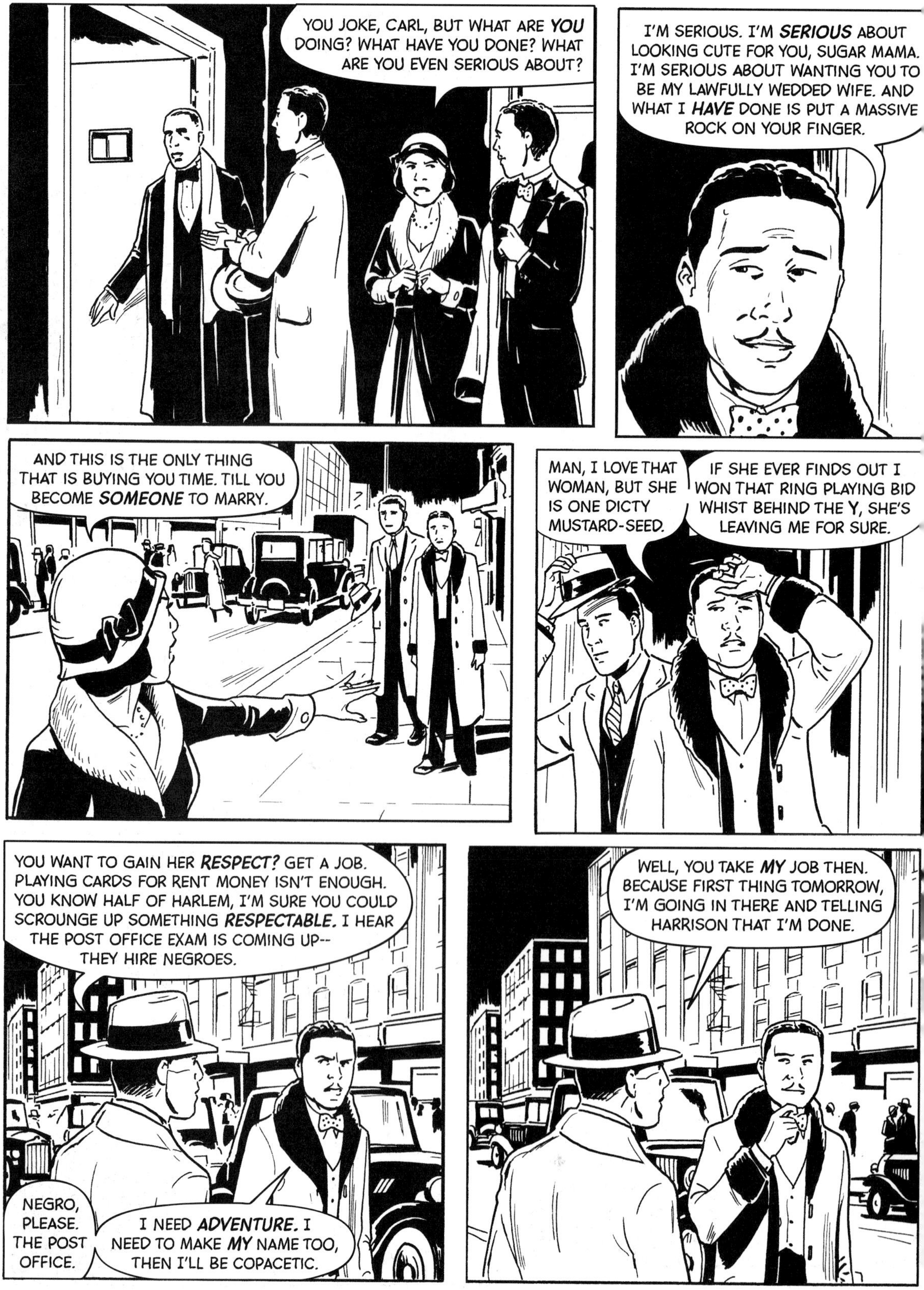
YOU JOKE, CARL, BUT WHAT ARE YOU DOING? WHAT HAVE YOU DONE? WHAT ARE YOU EVEN SERIOUS ABOUT?
I'M SERIOUS. I'M SERIOUS ABOUT LOOKING CUTE FOR YOU, SUGAR MAMA. I'M SERIOUS ABOUT WANTING YOU TO BE MY LAWFULLY WEDDED WIFE. AND WHAT I HAVE DONE IS PUT A MASSIVE ROCK ON YOUR FINGER.
AND THIS IS THE ONLY THING THAT IS BUYING YOU TIME. TILL YOU BECOME SOMEONE TO MARRY.
MAN, I LOVE THAT WOMAN, BUT SHE IS ONE DICTY MUSTARD-SEED.
IF SHE EVER FINDS OUT I WON THAT RING PLAYING BID WHIST BEHIND THE Y, SHE'S LEAVING ME FOR SURE.
YOU WANT TO GAIN HER RESPECT? GET A JOB. PLAYING CARDS FOR RENT MONEY ISN'T ENOUGH. YOU KNOW HALF OF HARLEM, I'M SURE YOU COULD SCROUNGE UP SOMETHING RESPECTABLE. I HEAR THE POST OFFICE EXAM IS COMING UP-- THEY HIRE NEGROES.
NEGRO, PLEASE. THE POST OFFICE.
I NEED ADVENTURE. I NEED TO MAKE MY NAME TOO, THEN I'LL BE COPACETIC.
WELL, YOU TAKE MY JOB THEN. BECAUSE FIRST THING TOMORROW, I'M GOING IN THERE AND TELLING HARRISON THAT I'M DONE.

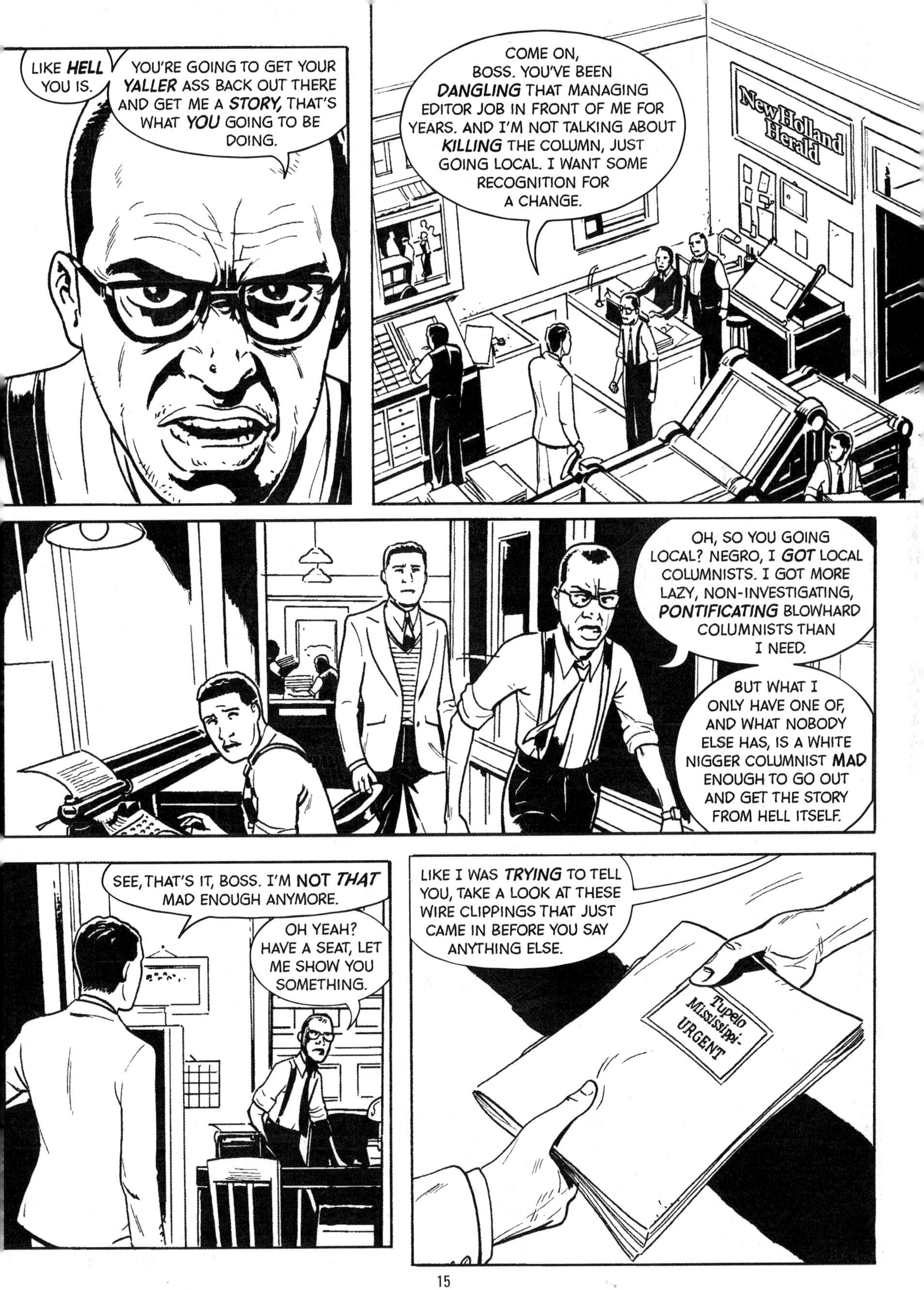
LIKE HELL YOU IS.
YOU'RE GOING TO GET YOUR YALLER ASS BACK OUT THERE AND GET ME A STORY, THAT'S WHAT YOU GOING TO BE DOING.
COME ON, BOSS. YOU'VE BEEN DANGLING THAT MANAGING EDITOR JOB IN FRONT OF ME FOR YEARS. AND I'M NOT TALKING ABOUT KILLING THE COLUMN, JUST GOING LOCAL. I WANT SOME RECOGNITION FOR A CHANGE.
New Holland Herald
OH, SO YOU GOING LOCAL? NEGRO, I GOT LOCAL COLUMNISTS. I GOT MORE LAZY, NON-INVESTIGATING, PONTIFICATING BLOWHARD COLUMNISTS THAN I NEED.
BUT WHAT I ONLY HAVE ONE OF, AND WHAT NOBODY ELSE HAS, IS A WHITE NIGGER COLUMNIST MAD ENOUGH TO GO OUT AND GET THE STORY FROM HELL ITSELF.
SEE, THAT'S IT, BOSS. I'M NOT THAT MAD ENOUGH ANYMORE.
OH YEAH? HAVE A SEAT, LET ME SHOW YOU SOMETHING.
LIKE I WAS TRYING TO TELL YOU, TAKE A LOOK AT THESE WIRE CLIPPINGS THAT JUST CAME IN BEFORE YOU SAY ANYTHING ELSE.
Tupelo Mississippi-URGENT

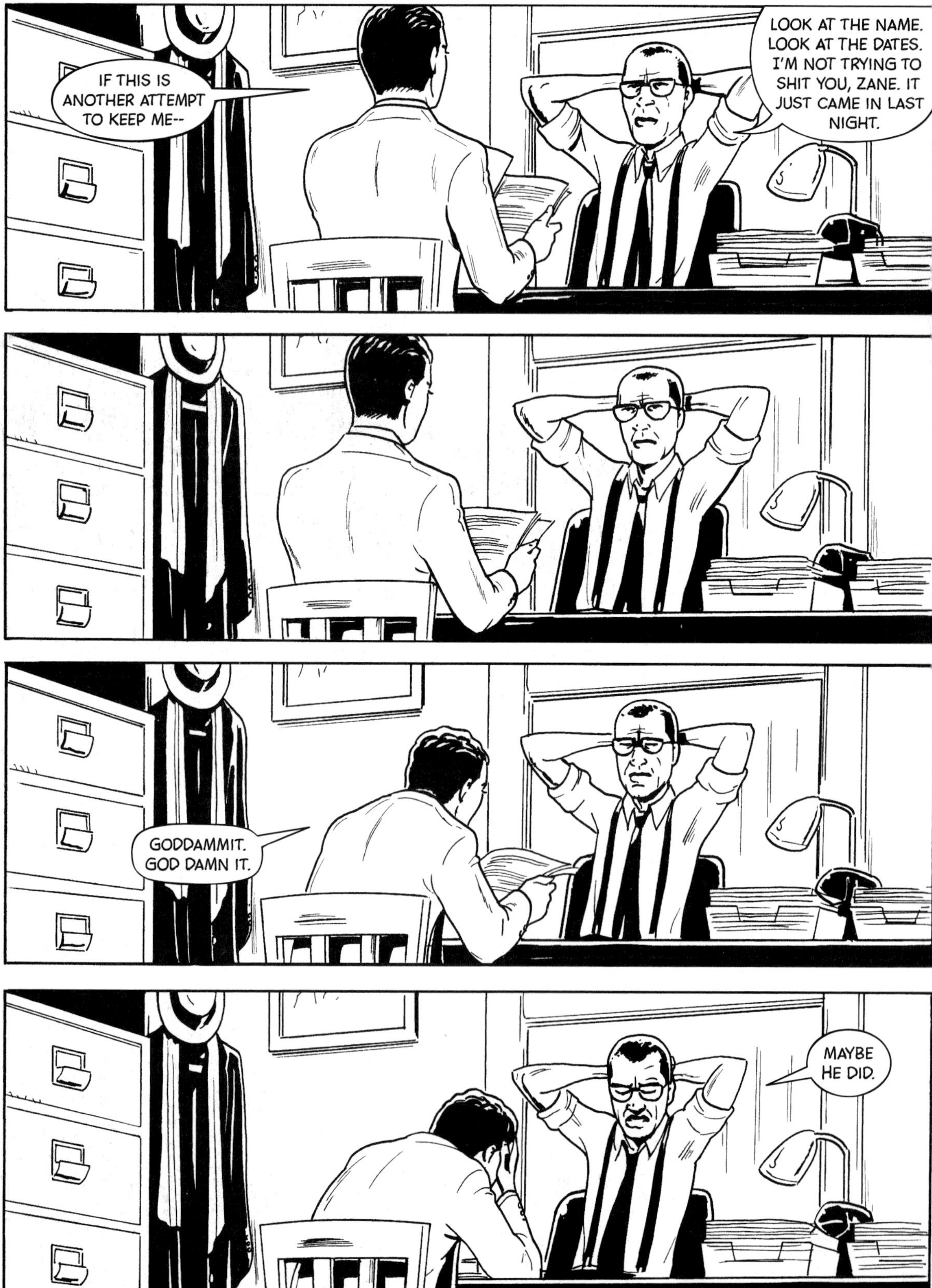
IF THIS IS ANOTHER ATTEMPT TO KEEP ME--
LOOK AT THE NAME. LOOK AT THE DATES. I'M NOT TRYING TO SHIT YOU, ZANE. IT JUST CAME IN LAST NIGHT.
GODDAMMIT. GOD DAMN IT.
MAYBE HE DID.

ALL RIGHT, FINE, I'M ON THIS *LAST* STORY. BUT THIS CHANGES *NOTHING.* WHEN I COME BACK, I BETTER HAVE AN OFFICE. AND IT BETTER SAY *MANAGING EDITOR* ON THE DOOR.

MAKE IT BACK, AND MAKE IT BACK SAFE, AND I'LL GIVE YOU THAT *AND* A COLUMN, WITH YOUR *PICTURE* ON THE FRONT.

BUT NOT A RAISE.

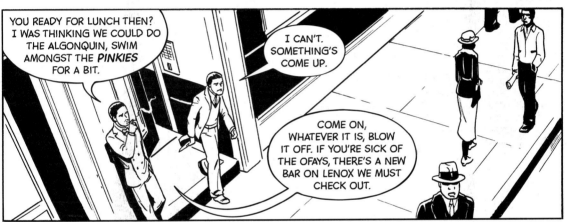

YOU READY FOR LUNCH THEN? I WAS THINKING WE COULD DO THE ALGONQUIN, SWIM AMONGST THE *PINKIES* FOR A BIT.

I CAN'T. SOMETHING'S COME UP.

COME ON, WHATEVER IT IS, BLOW IT OFF. IF YOU'RE SICK OF THE OFAYS, THERE'S A NEW BAR ON LENOX WE MUST CHECK OUT.

LIFE IS NOT ALL BAR STOOLS AND RENT PARTIES, CARL. SOMETIMES A MAN HAS TO *DO* SOMETHING, AND RIGHT NOW I HAVE TO BE ON THE 8:13 CAROLINIAN EN ROUTE TO YAZOO CITY.

HEY, I DON'T NEED THAT FROM YOU, TOO! I'M ABOUT TO MAKE *MOVES,* SLICK! YOU WATCH ME!

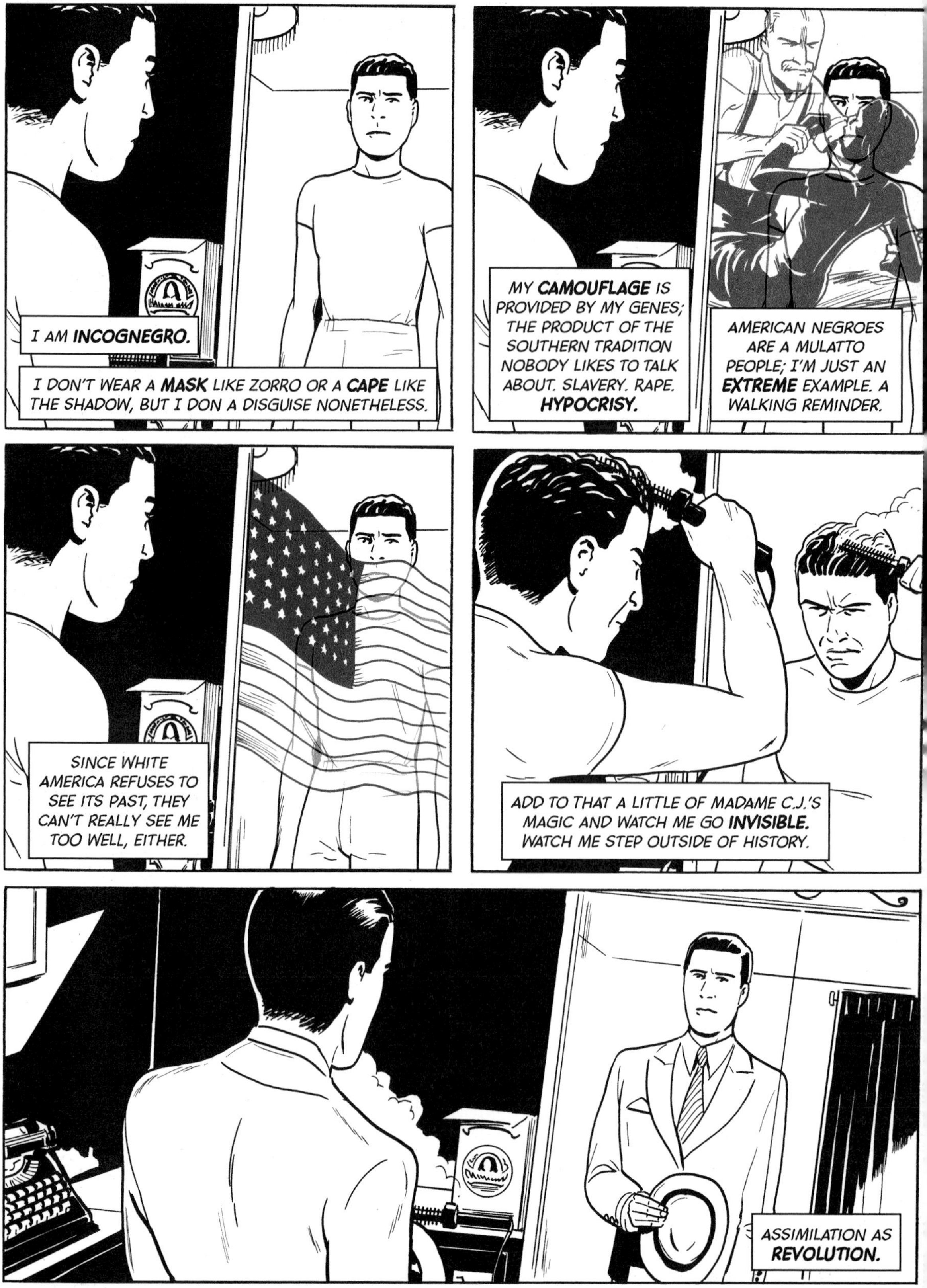

I AM INCOGNEGRO.
I DON'T WEAR A MASK LIKE ZORRO OR A CAPE LIKE THE SHADOW, BUT I DON A DISGUISE NONETHELESS.
MY CAMOUFLAGE IS PROVIDED BY MY GENES; THE PRODUCT OF THE SOUTHERN TRADITION NOBODY LIKES TO TALK ABOUT. SLAVERY. RAPE. HYPOCRISY.
AMERICAN NEGROES ARE A MULATTO PEOPLE; I'M JUST AN EXTREME EXAMPLE. A WALKING REMINDER.
SINCE WHITE AMERICA REFUSES TO SEE ITS PAST, THEY CAN'T REALLY SEE ME TOO WELL, EITHER.
ADD TO THAT A LITTLE OF MADAME C.J.'S MAGIC AND WATCH ME GO INVISIBLE. WATCH ME STEP OUTSIDE OF HISTORY.
ASSIMILATION AS REVOLUTION.

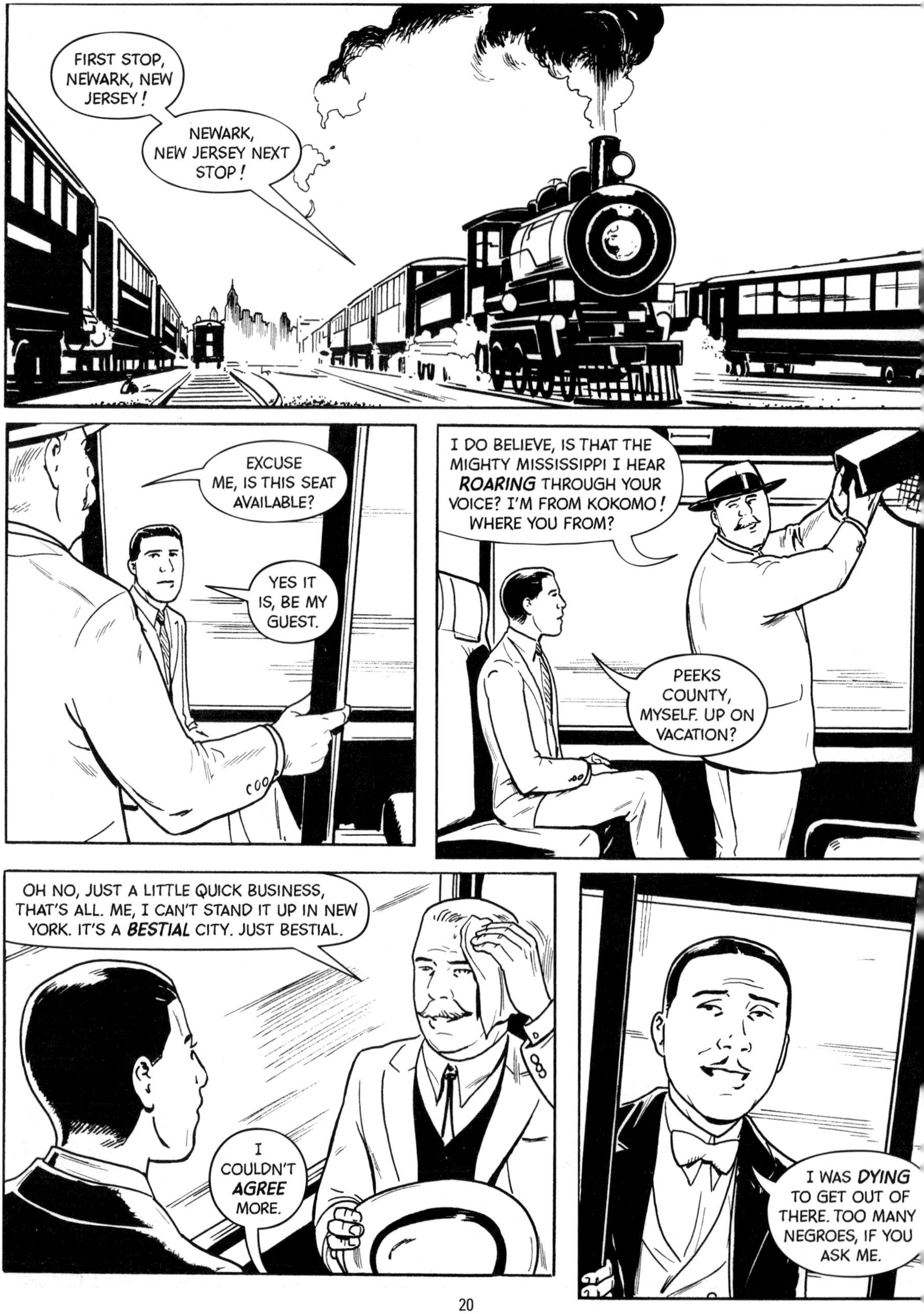
FIRST STOP, NEWARK, NEW JERSEY!
NEWARK, NEW JERSEY NEXT STOP!
EXCUSE ME, IS THIS SEAT AVAILABLE?
YES IT IS, BE MY GUEST.
I DO BELIEVE, IS THAT THE MIGHTY MISSISSIPPI I HEAR ROARING THROUGH YOUR VOICE? I'M FROM KOKOMO! WHERE YOU FROM?
PEEKS COUNTY, MYSELF. UP ON VACATION?
OH NO, JUST A LITTLE QUICK BUSINESS, THAT'S ALL. ME, I CAN'T STAND IT UP IN NEW YORK. IT'S A BESTIAL CITY. JUST BESTIAL.
I COULDN'T AGREE MORE.
I WAS DYING TO GET OUT OF THERE. TOO MANY NEGROES, IF YOU ASK ME.

*ARE YOU A KLANSMAN?

*A KLANSMAN I AM

24

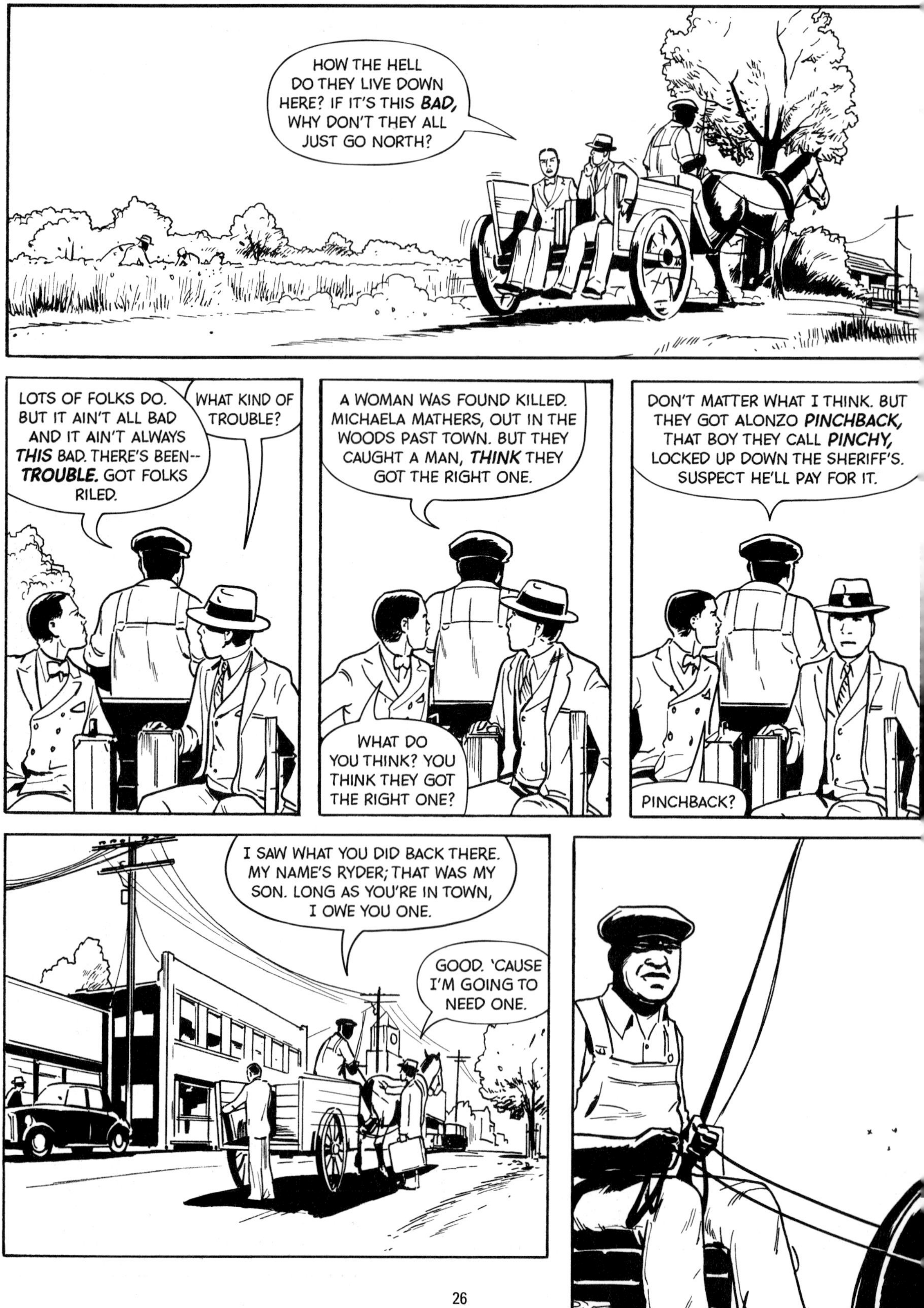
HOW THE HELL DO THEY LIVE DOWN HERE? IF IT'S THIS BAD, WHY DON'T THEY ALL JUST GO NORTH?
LOTS OF FOLKS DO. BUT IT AIN'T ALL BAD AND IT AIN'T ALWAYS THIS BAD. THERE'S BEEN-- TROUBLE. GOT FOLKS RILED.
WHAT KIND OF TROUBLE?
A WOMAN WAS FOUND KILLED. MICHAELA MATHERS, OUT IN THE WOODS PAST TOWN. BUT THEY CAUGHT A MAN, THINK THEY GOT THE RIGHT ONE.
WHAT DO YOU THINK? YOU THINK THEY GOT THE RIGHT ONE?
DON'T MATTER WHAT I THINK. BUT THEY GOT ALONZO PINCHBACK, THAT BOY THEY CALL PINCHY, LOCKED UP DOWN THE SHERIFF'S. SUSPECT HE'LL PAY FOR IT.
PINCHBACK?
I SAW WHAT YOU DID BACK THERE. MY NAME'S RYDER; THAT WAS MY SON. LONG AS YOU'RE IN TOWN, I OWE YOU ONE.
GOOD. 'CAUSE I'M GOING TO NEED ONE.

PINCHBACK? HE SAID PINCHBACK, AM I RIGHT? WHAT THE HELL'S GOING ON HERE?

I'LL TELL YOU LATER. JUST GO AND FIND US SOMEPLACE TO STAY. SOMEPLACE *QUIET*, OKAY?

SOMEPLACE *LOW PROFILE*. ANYBODY ASKS ABOUT ME, HINT THAT I'M FROM THE KLAN; THAT SHOULD COVER US FOR NOW.

AND CARL, CUT THE SOUTHERN ACCENT; IT'S *HORRENDOUS*. JUST STAY OUT OF TROUBLE AND I'LL MEET YOU BACK AROUND HERE IN AN HOUR.

COME ON, Z. A *LITTLE* TROUBLE MAKES THE WORLD GO AROUND.

I DON'T CARE WHO YOU ARE OR WHAT YOU'RE *SELLING*. WE GOT ENOUGH GOING ON AROUND HERE WITHOUT ANY *MORE* BEING BROUGHT IN.

GOOD TO MEET YOU TOO SIR, BUT YOU BEST LISTEN TO ME OR YOU MIGHT NOT GET A CHOICE. *AYAK?*

SHERIFF, DEPUTY, CATCH RECORD STRIPER ON LUNCH

AY-*WHAT?* LOOK, I'M ALREADY SHORT MY *DEPUTY*, SO I DON'T HAVE TIME FOR THIS SHIT. WHAT DO YOU WANT?

27

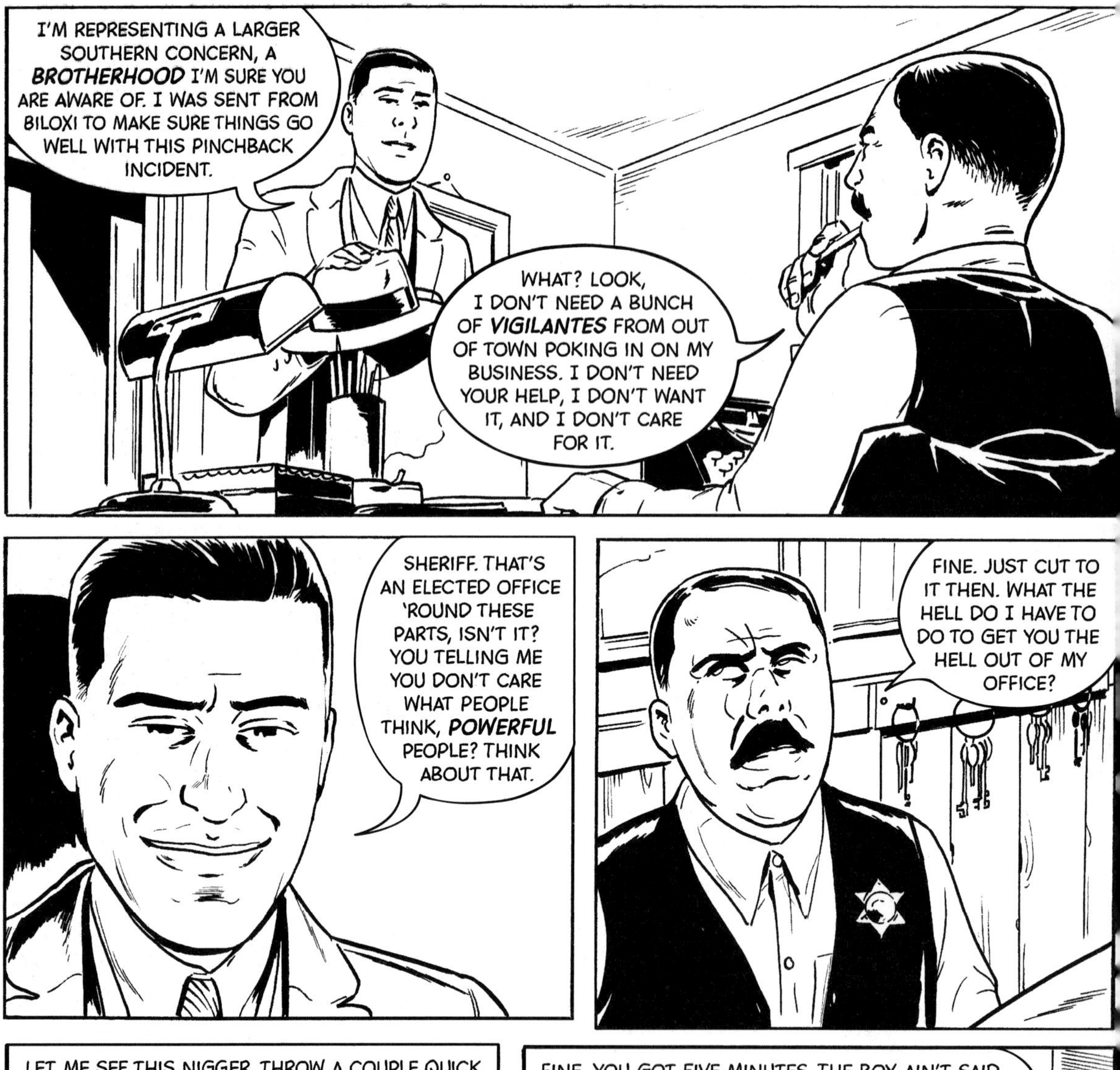
I'M REPRESENTING A LARGER SOUTHERN CONCERN, A **BROTHERHOOD** I'M SURE YOU ARE AWARE OF. I WAS SENT FROM BILOXI TO MAKE SURE THINGS GO WELL WITH THIS PINCHBACK INCIDENT.
WHAT? LOOK, I DON'T NEED A BUNCH OF **VIGILANTES** FROM OUT OF TOWN POKING IN ON MY BUSINESS. I DON'T NEED YOUR HELP, I DON'T WANT IT, AND I DON'T CARE FOR IT.
SHERIFF. THAT'S AN ELECTED OFFICE 'ROUND THESE PARTS, ISN'T IT? YOU TELLING ME YOU DON'T CARE WHAT PEOPLE THINK, **POWERFUL** PEOPLE? THINK ABOUT THAT.
FINE. JUST CUT TO IT THEN. WHAT THE HELL DO I HAVE TO DO TO GET YOU THE HELL OUT OF MY OFFICE?
LET ME SEE THIS NIGGER, THROW A COUPLE QUICK **QUESTIONS** AT HIM MYSELF. THEN I CAN GO BACK AND TELL MY PEOPLE, SPREAD THE WORD THAT YOU'RE DOING A GOOD JOB, AND **EVERYONE'S** HAPPY.
YOU MIGHT EVEN AVOID THE MOB THAT I SEE IS BUILDING OUT THERE.
FINE. YOU GOT FIVE MINUTES. THE BOY AIN'T SAID HARDLY **NOTHING** FOR THE LAST WEEK, SO YOU SEE HOW YOUR LUCK'S ANY DIFFERENT.

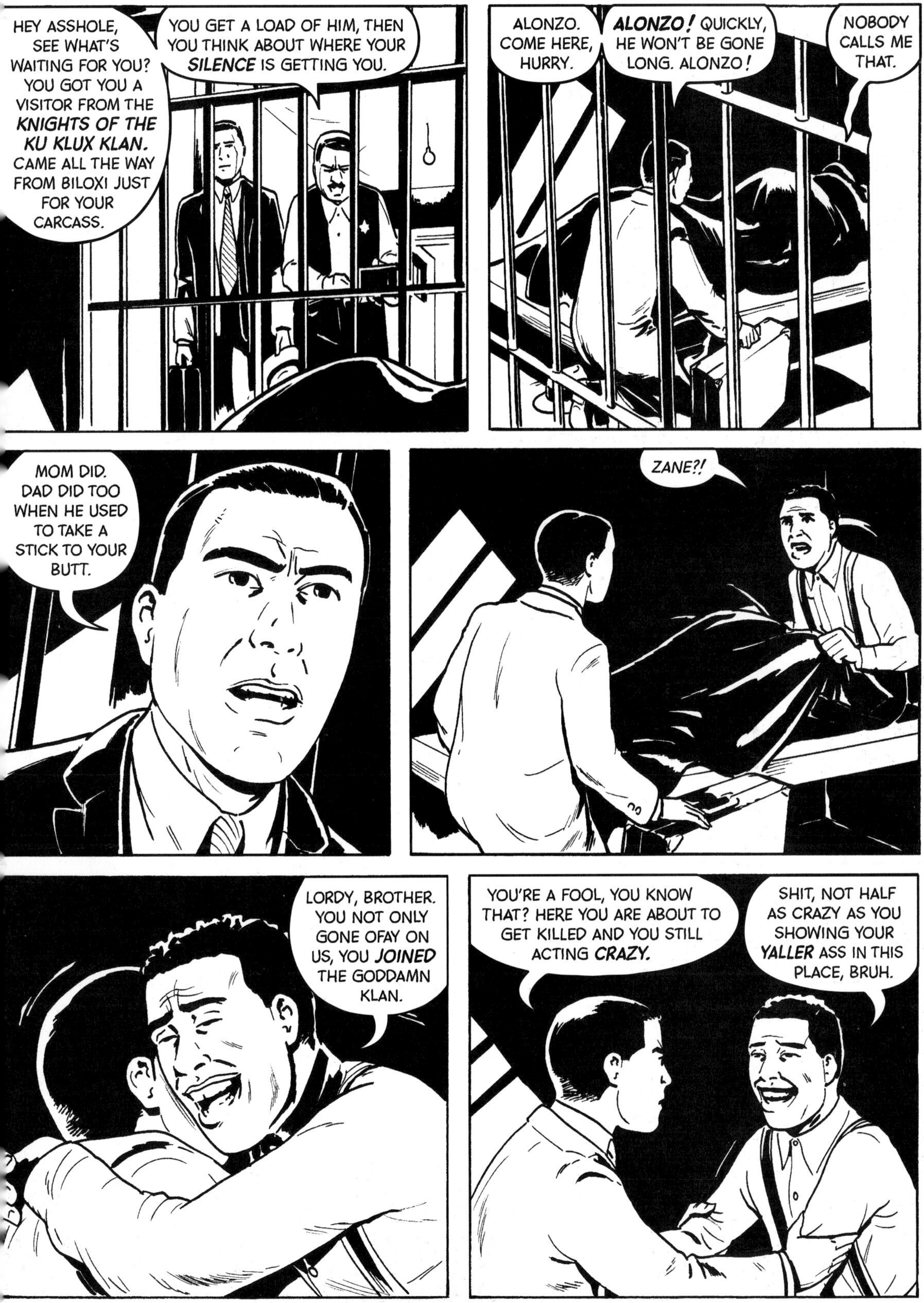

HEY ASSHOLE, SEE WHAT'S WAITING FOR YOU? YOU GOT YOU A VISITOR FROM THE **KNIGHTS OF THE KU KLUX KLAN.** CAME ALL THE WAY FROM BILOXI JUST FOR YOUR CARCASS.
YOU GET A LOAD OF HIM, THEN YOU THINK ABOUT WHERE YOUR **SILENCE** IS GETTING YOU.
ALONZO. COME HERE, HURRY.
ALONZO! QUICKLY, HE WON'T BE GONE LONG. ALONZO!
NOBODY CALLS ME THAT.
MOM DID. DAD DID TOO WHEN HE USED TO TAKE A STICK TO YOUR BUTT.
ZANE?!
LORDY, BROTHER. YOU NOT ONLY GONE OFAY ON US, YOU **JOINED** THE GODDAMN KLAN.
YOU'RE A FOOL, YOU KNOW THAT? HERE YOU ARE ABOUT TO GET KILLED AND YOU STILL ACTING **CRAZY.**
SHIT, NOT HALF AS CRAZY AS YOU SHOWING YOUR **YALLER** ASS IN THIS PLACE, BRUH.

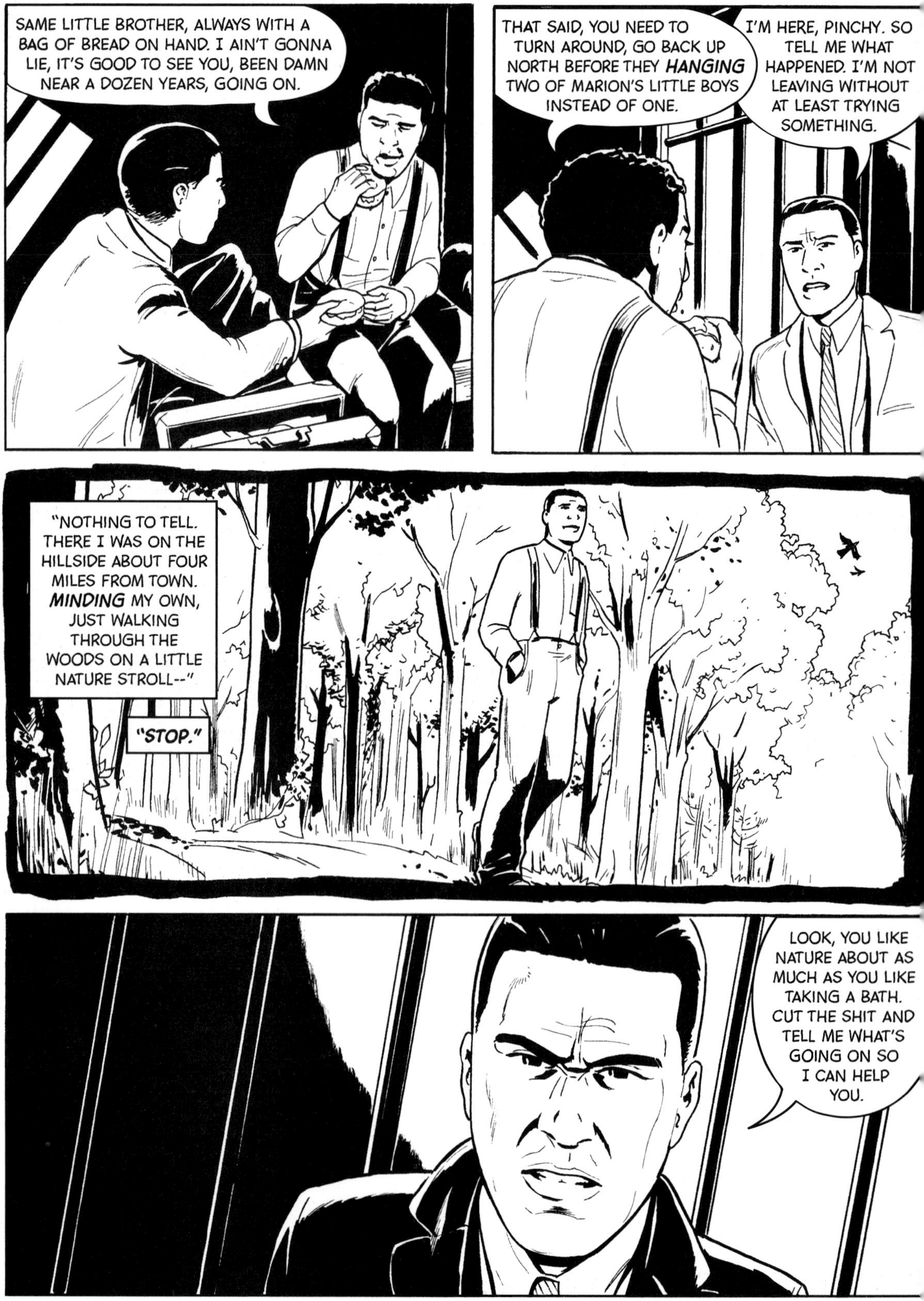

SAME LITTLE BROTHER, ALWAYS WITH A BAG OF BREAD ON HAND. I AIN'T GONNA LIE, IT'S GOOD TO SEE YOU, BEEN DAMN NEAR A DOZEN YEARS, GOING ON.
THAT SAID, YOU NEED TO TURN AROUND, GO BACK UP NORTH BEFORE THEY HANGING TWO OF MARION'S LITTLE BOYS INSTEAD OF ONE.
I'M HERE, PINCHY. SO TELL ME WHAT HAPPENED. I'M NOT LEAVING WITHOUT AT LEAST TRYING SOMETHING.
"NOTHING TO TELL. THERE I WAS ON THE HILLSIDE ABOUT FOUR MILES FROM TOWN. MINDING MY OWN, JUST WALKING THROUGH THE WOODS ON A LITTLE NATURE STROLL--"
"STOP."
LOOK, YOU LIKE NATURE ABOUT AS MUCH AS YOU LIKE TAKING A BATH. CUT THE SHIT AND TELL ME WHAT'S GOING ON SO I CAN HELP YOU.

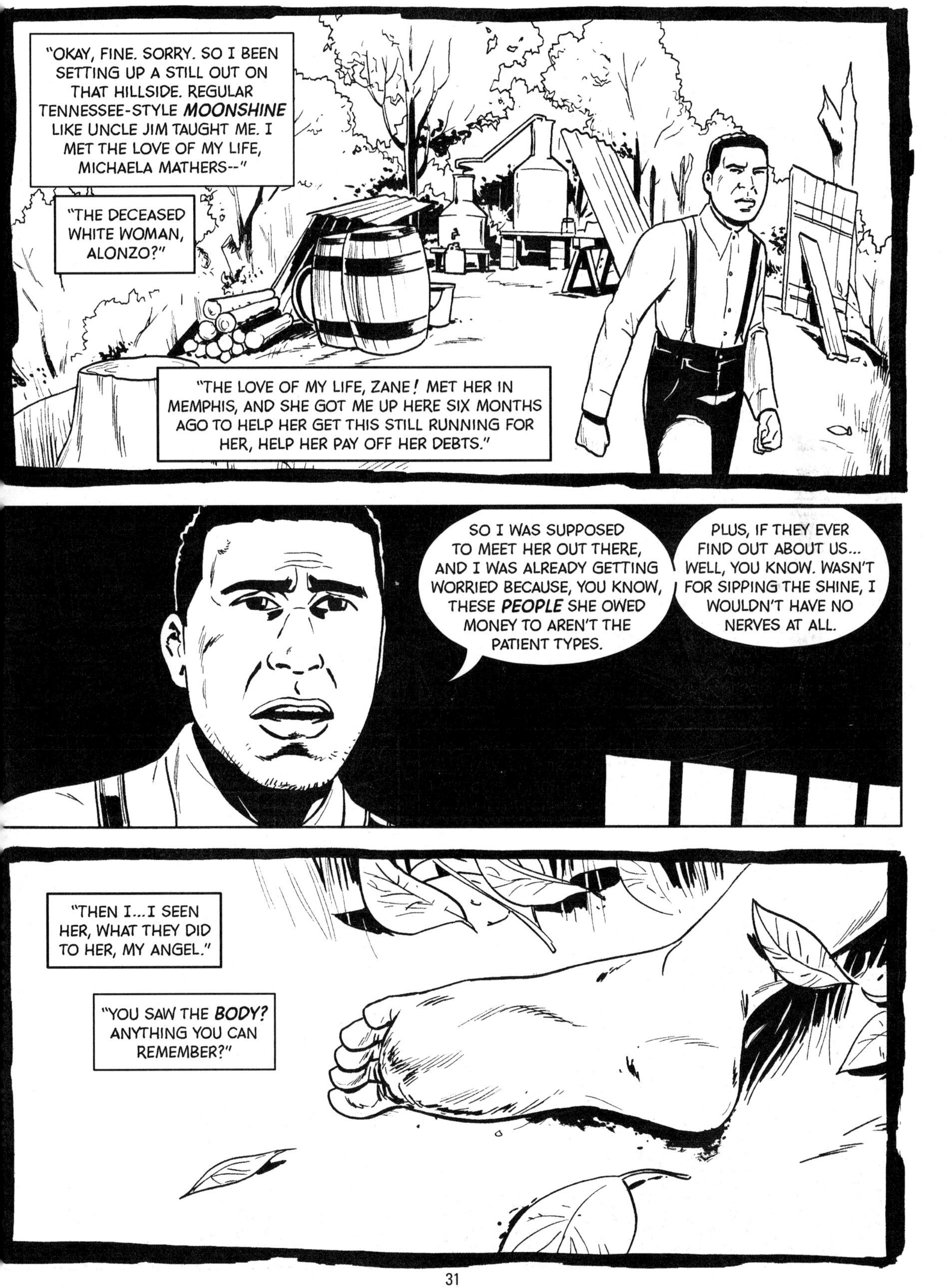
"OKAY, FINE. SORRY. SO I BEEN SETTING UP A STILL OUT ON THAT HILLSIDE. REGULAR TENNESSEE-STYLE MOONSHINE LIKE UNCLE JIM TAUGHT ME. I MET THE LOVE OF MY LIFE, MICHAELA MATHERS--"
"THE DECEASED WHITE WOMAN, ALONZO?"
"THE LOVE OF MY LIFE, ZANE! MET HER IN MEMPHIS, AND SHE GOT ME UP HERE SIX MONTHS AGO TO HELP HER GET THIS STILL RUNNING FOR HER, HELP HER PAY OFF HER DEBTS."
SO I WAS SUPPOSED TO MEET HER OUT THERE, AND I WAS ALREADY GETTING WORRIED BECAUSE, YOU KNOW, THESE PEOPLE SHE OWED MONEY TO AREN'T THE PATIENT TYPES.
PLUS, IF THEY EVER FIND OUT ABOUT US... WELL, YOU KNOW. WASN'T FOR SIPPING THE SHINE, I WOULDN'T HAVE NO NERVES AT ALL.
"THEN I...I SEEN HER, WHAT THEY DID TO HER, MY ANGEL."
"YOU SAW THE BODY? ANYTHING YOU CAN REMEMBER?"

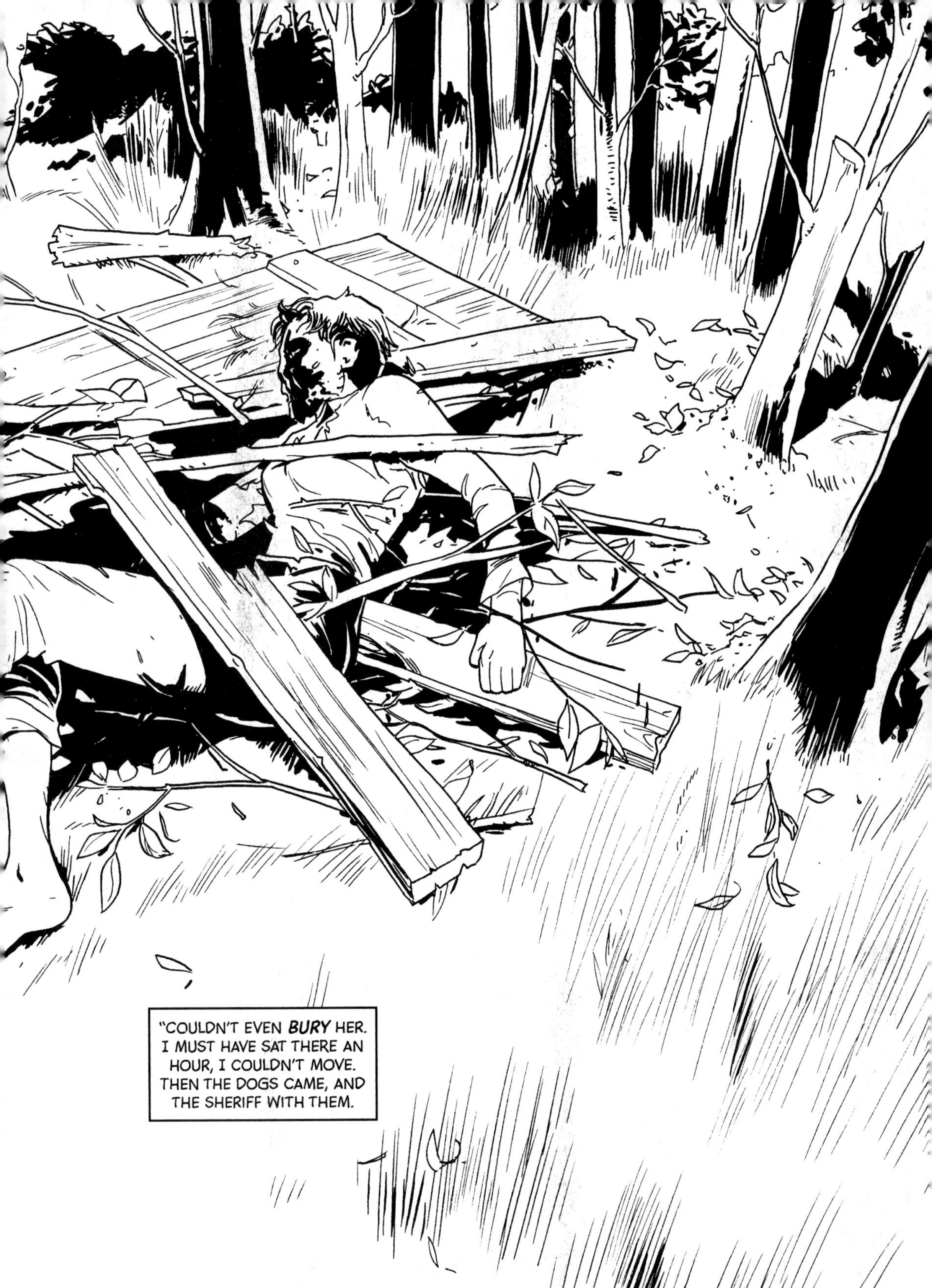
"COULDN'T EVEN **BURY** HER. I MUST HAVE SAT THERE AN HOUR, I COULDN'T MOVE. THEN THE DOGS CAME, AND THE SHERIFF WITH THEM.

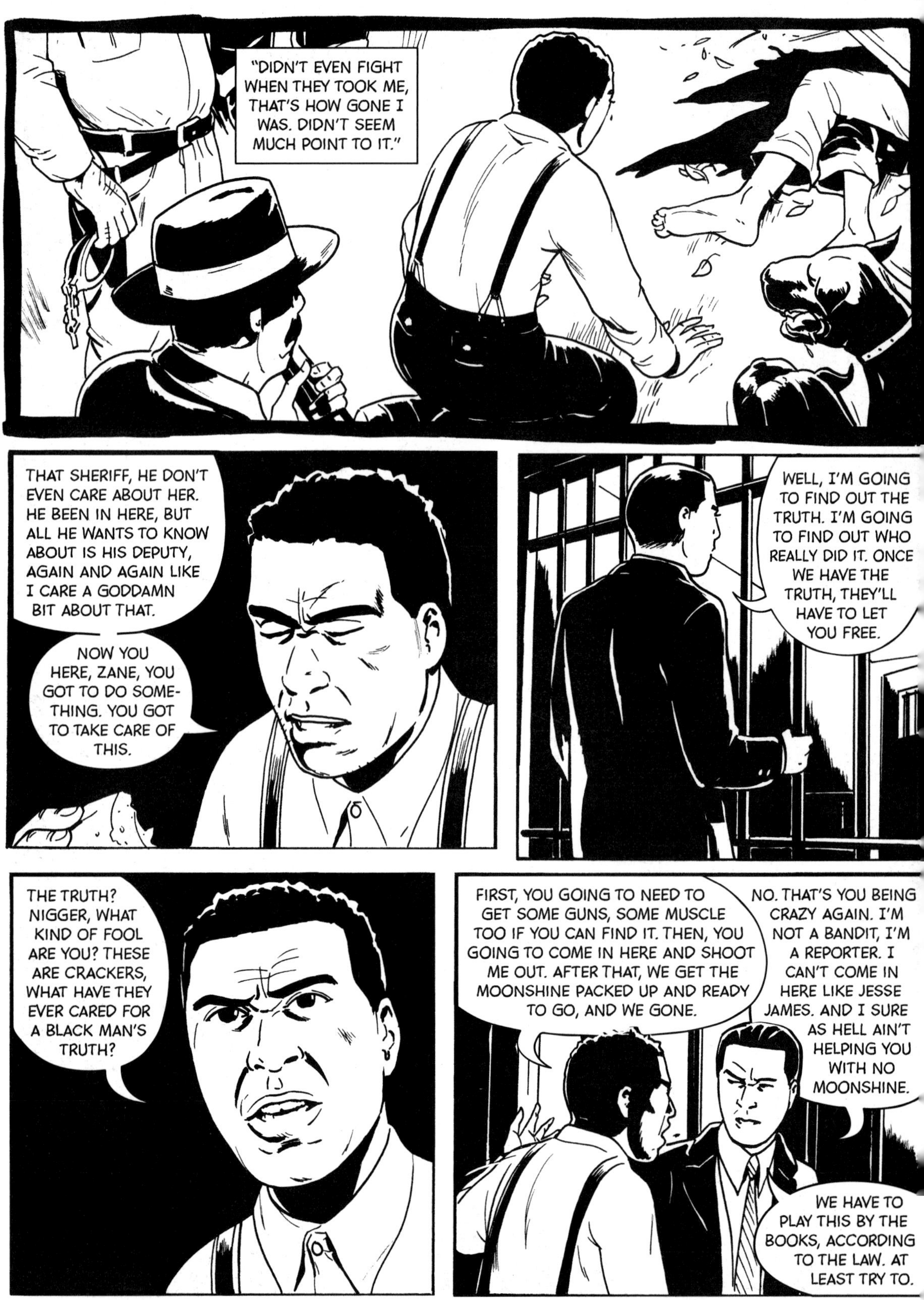
"DIDN'T EVEN FIGHT WHEN THEY TOOK ME, THAT'S HOW GONE I WAS. DIDN'T SEEM MUCH POINT TO IT."
THAT SHERIFF, HE DON'T EVEN CARE ABOUT HER. HE BEEN IN HERE, BUT ALL HE WANTS TO KNOW ABOUT IS HIS DEPUTY, AGAIN AND AGAIN LIKE I CARE A GODDAMN BIT ABOUT THAT.
NOW YOU HERE, ZANE, YOU GOT TO DO SOME-THING. YOU GOT TO TAKE CARE OF THIS.
WELL, I'M GOING TO FIND OUT THE TRUTH. I'M GOING TO FIND OUT WHO REALLY DID IT. ONCE WE HAVE THE TRUTH, THEY'LL HAVE TO LET YOU FREE.
THE TRUTH? NIGGER, WHAT KIND OF FOOL ARE YOU? THESE ARE CRACKERS, WHAT HAVE THEY EVER CARED FOR A BLACK MAN'S TRUTH?
FIRST, YOU GOING TO NEED TO GET SOME GUNS, SOME MUSCLE TOO IF YOU CAN FIND IT. THEN, YOU GOING TO COME IN HERE AND SHOOT ME OUT. AFTER THAT, WE GET THE MOONSHINE PACKED UP AND READY TO GO, AND WE GONE.
NO. THAT'S YOU BEING CRAZY AGAIN. I'M NOT A BANDIT, I'M A REPORTER. I CAN'T COME IN HERE LIKE JESSE JAMES. AND I SURE AS HELL AIN'T HELPING YOU WITH NO MOONSHINE.
WE HAVE TO PLAY THIS BY THE BOOKS, ACCORDING TO THE LAW. AT LEAST TRY TO.

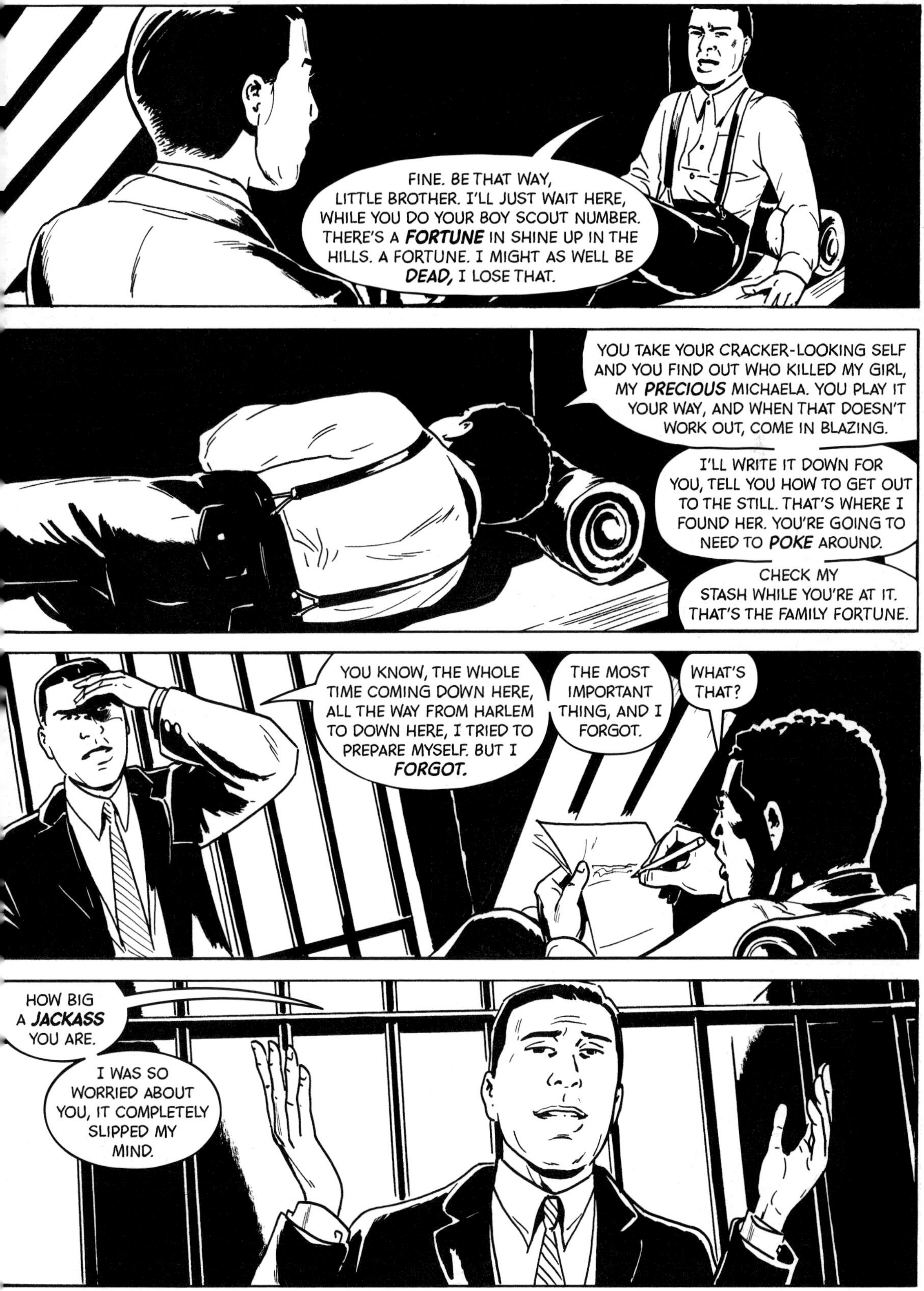
FINE. BE THAT WAY, LITTLE BROTHER. I'LL JUST WAIT HERE, WHILE YOU DO YOUR BOY SCOUT NUMBER. THERE'S A ***FORTUNE*** IN SHINE UP IN THE HILLS. A FORTUNE. I MIGHT AS WELL BE ***DEAD,*** I LOSE THAT.
YOU TAKE YOUR CRACKER-LOOKING SELF AND YOU FIND OUT WHO KILLED MY GIRL, MY ***PRECIOUS*** MICHAELA. YOU PLAY IT YOUR WAY, AND WHEN THAT DOESN'T WORK OUT, COME IN BLAZING.
I'LL WRITE IT DOWN FOR YOU, TELL YOU HOW TO GET OUT TO THE STILL. THAT'S WHERE I FOUND HER. YOU'RE GOING TO NEED TO ***POKE*** AROUND.
CHECK MY STASH WHILE YOU'RE AT IT. THAT'S THE FAMILY FORTUNE.
YOU KNOW, THE WHOLE TIME COMING DOWN HERE, ALL THE WAY FROM HARLEM TO DOWN HERE, I TRIED TO PREPARE MYSELF. BUT I ***FORGOT.***
THE MOST IMPORTANT THING, AND I FORGOT.
WHAT'S THAT?
HOW BIG A ***JACKASS*** YOU ARE.
I WAS SO WORRIED ABOUT YOU, IT COMPLETELY SLIPPED MY MIND.

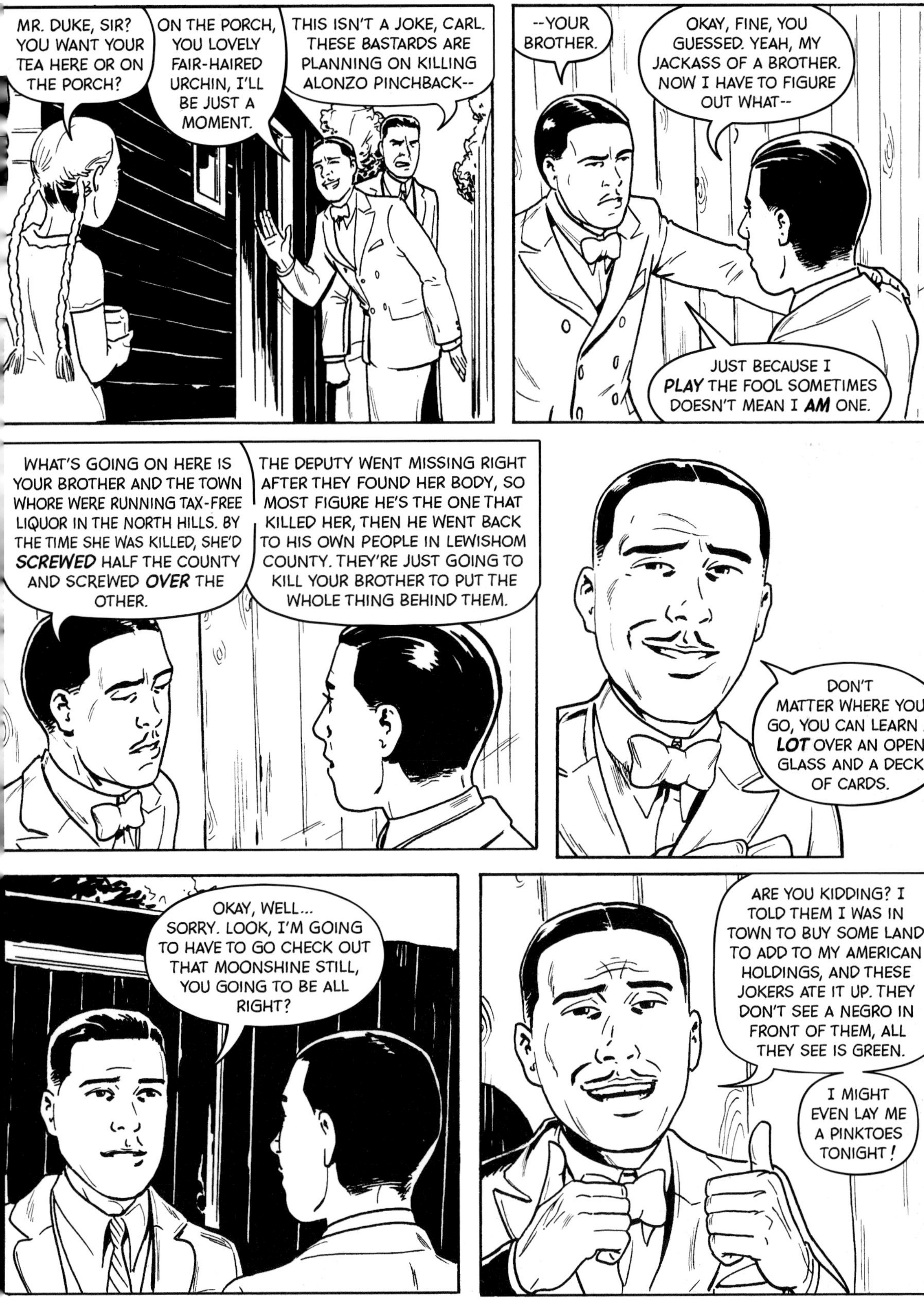
MR. DUKE, SIR? YOU WANT YOUR TEA HERE OR ON THE PORCH?
ON THE PORCH, YOU LOVELY FAIR-HAIRED URCHIN, I'LL BE JUST A MOMENT.
THIS ISN'T A JOKE, CARL. THESE BASTARDS ARE PLANNING ON KILLING ALONZO PINCHBACK--
--YOUR BROTHER.
OKAY, FINE, YOU GUESSED. YEAH, MY JACKASS OF A BROTHER. NOW I HAVE TO FIGURE OUT WHAT--
JUST BECAUSE I PLAY THE FOOL SOMETIMES DOESN'T MEAN I AM ONE.
WHAT'S GOING ON HERE IS YOUR BROTHER AND THE TOWN WHORE WERE RUNNING TAX-FREE LIQUOR IN THE NORTH HILLS. BY THE TIME SHE WAS KILLED, SHE'D SCREWED HALF THE COUNTY AND SCREWED OVER THE OTHER.
THE DEPUTY WENT MISSING RIGHT AFTER THEY FOUND HER BODY, SO MOST FIGURE HE'S THE ONE THAT KILLED HER, THEN HE WENT BACK TO HIS OWN PEOPLE IN LEWISHOM COUNTY. THEY'RE JUST GOING TO KILL YOUR BROTHER TO PUT THE WHOLE THING BEHIND THEM.
DON'T MATTER WHERE YOU GO, YOU CAN LEARN A LOT OVER AN OPEN GLASS AND A DECK OF CARDS.
OKAY, WELL... SORRY. LOOK, I'M GOING TO HAVE TO GO CHECK OUT THAT MOONSHINE STILL, YOU GOING TO BE ALL RIGHT?
ARE YOU KIDDING? I TOLD THEM I WAS IN TOWN TO BUY SOME LAND TO ADD TO MY AMERICAN HOLDINGS, AND THESE JOKERS ATE IT UP. THEY DON'T SEE A NEGRO IN FRONT OF THEM, ALL THEY SEE IS GREEN.
I MIGHT EVEN LAY ME A PINKTOES TONIGHT!

Take Bloom Street to the north of town. Walk three miles past that.

Once your feet start to **throbbing**, you'll see an old lady selling bait, that's where you want to go.

Don't talk to her, 'cause she's **touched**. Don't nobody even fish around them parts, but there she is trying to sell minnows.

Behind her shack, that's where you find the trail to my still.

Just make a left at the dead dog. Michaela done that, have mercy on her soul. To keep the kids away.

38

POWWW

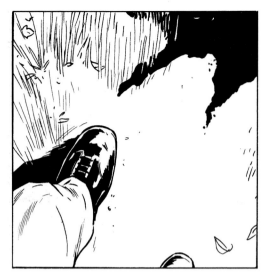

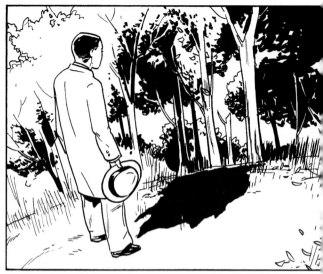

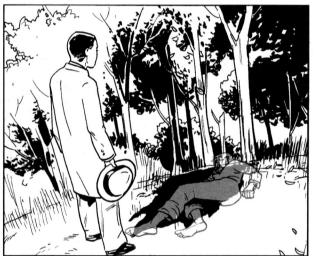

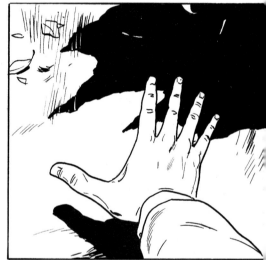

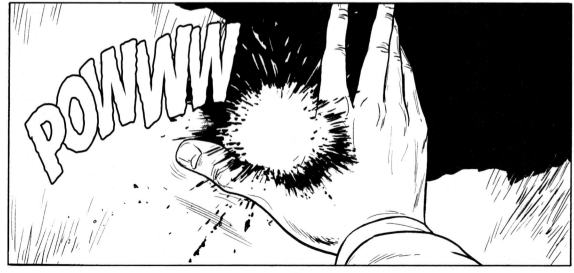

42

That shine. It's a masterpiece. Delicate. Love's flower.

RIIIIP

Creation itself's.

Alcohol so pure, you could drive your auto-mobile on it.

OH LORDY JESUS, I'M ON FIRE! HELP! HELP!

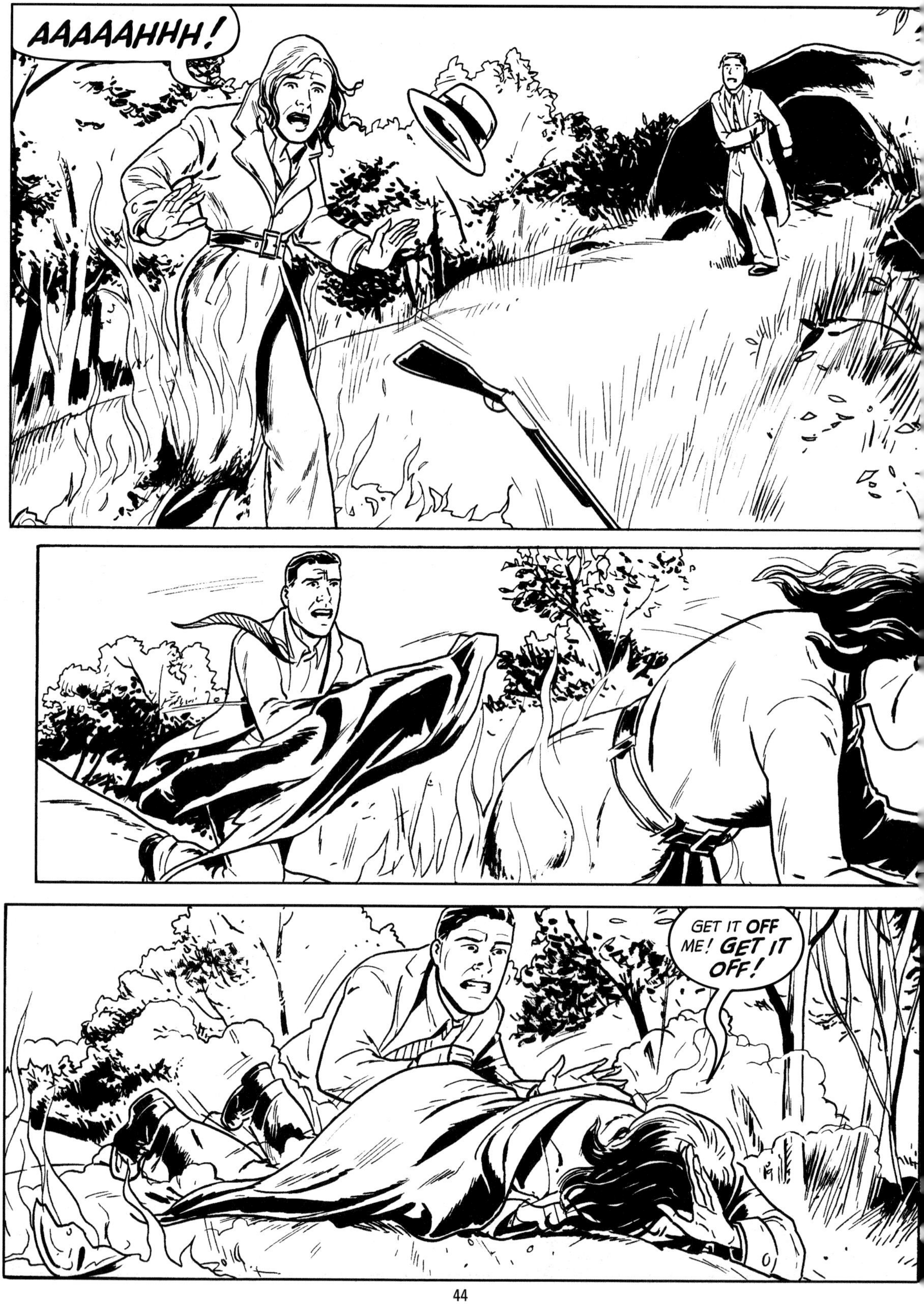
AAAAAHHH!
GET IT OFF ME! GET IT OFF!

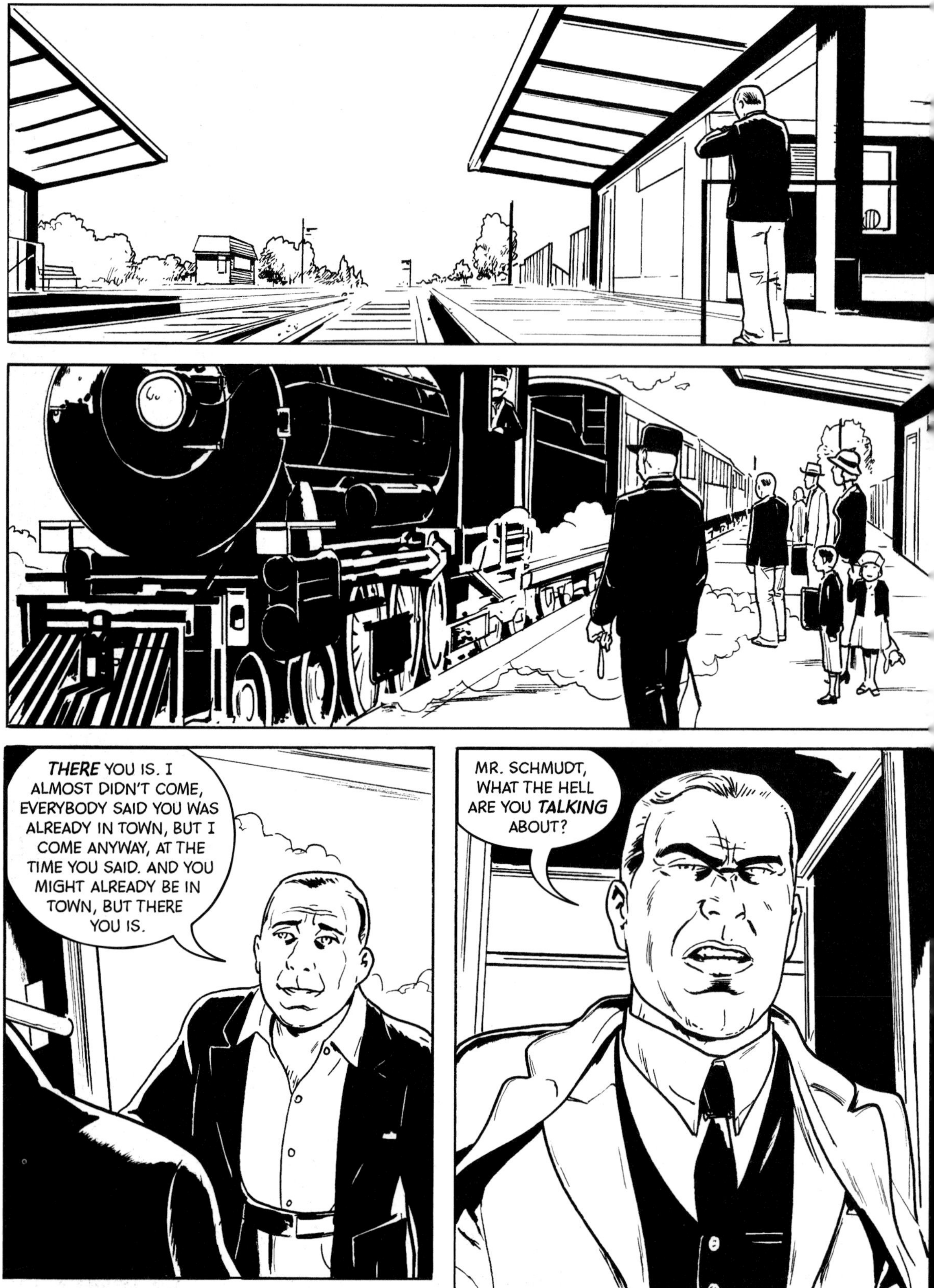

THERE YOU IS. I ALMOST DIDN'T COME, EVERYBODY SAID YOU WAS ALREADY IN TOWN, BUT I COME ANYWAY, AT THE TIME YOU SAID. AND YOU MIGHT ALREADY BE IN TOWN, BUT THERE YOU IS.
MR. SCHMUDT, WHAT THE HELL ARE YOU *TALKING* ABOUT?

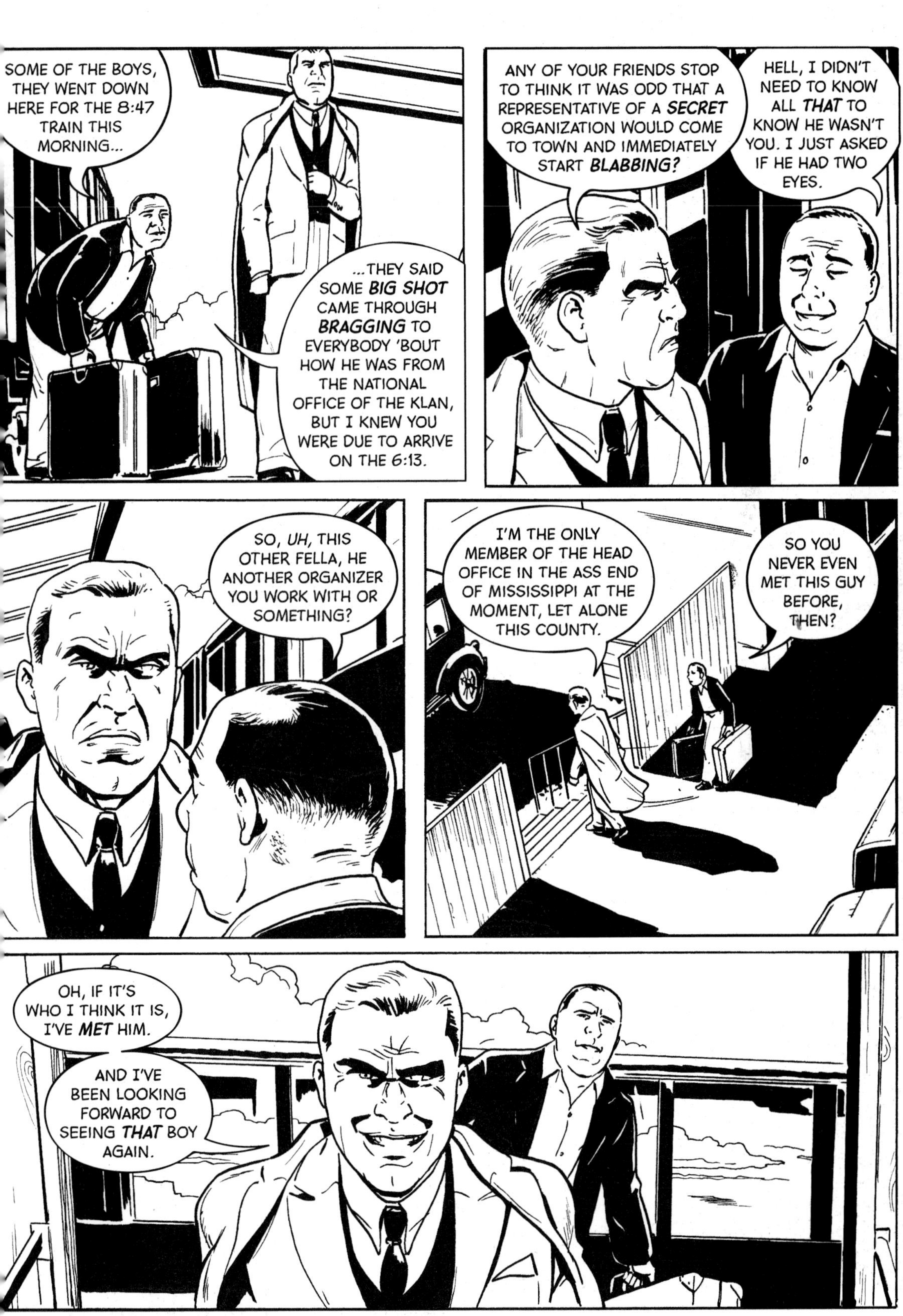
SOME OF THE BOYS, THEY WENT DOWN HERE FOR THE 8:47 TRAIN THIS MORNING...
...THEY SAID SOME BIG SHOT CAME THROUGH BRAGGING TO EVERYBODY 'BOUT HOW HE WAS FROM THE NATIONAL OFFICE OF THE KLAN, BUT I KNEW YOU WERE DUE TO ARRIVE ON THE 6:13.
ANY OF YOUR FRIENDS STOP TO THINK IT WAS ODD THAT A REPRESENTATIVE OF A SECRET ORGANIZATION WOULD COME TO TOWN AND IMMEDIATELY START BLABBING?
HELL, I DIDN'T NEED TO KNOW ALL THAT TO KNOW HE WASN'T YOU. I JUST ASKED IF HE HAD TWO EYES.
SO, UH, THIS OTHER FELLA, HE ANOTHER ORGANIZER YOU WORK WITH OR SOMETHING?
I'M THE ONLY MEMBER OF THE HEAD OFFICE IN THE ASS END OF MISSISSIPPI AT THE MOMENT, LET ALONE THIS COUNTY.
SO YOU NEVER EVEN MET THIS GUY BEFORE, THEN?
OH, IF IT'S WHO I THINK IT IS, I'VE MET HIM.
AND I'VE BEEN LOOKING FORWARD TO SEEING THAT BOY AGAIN.

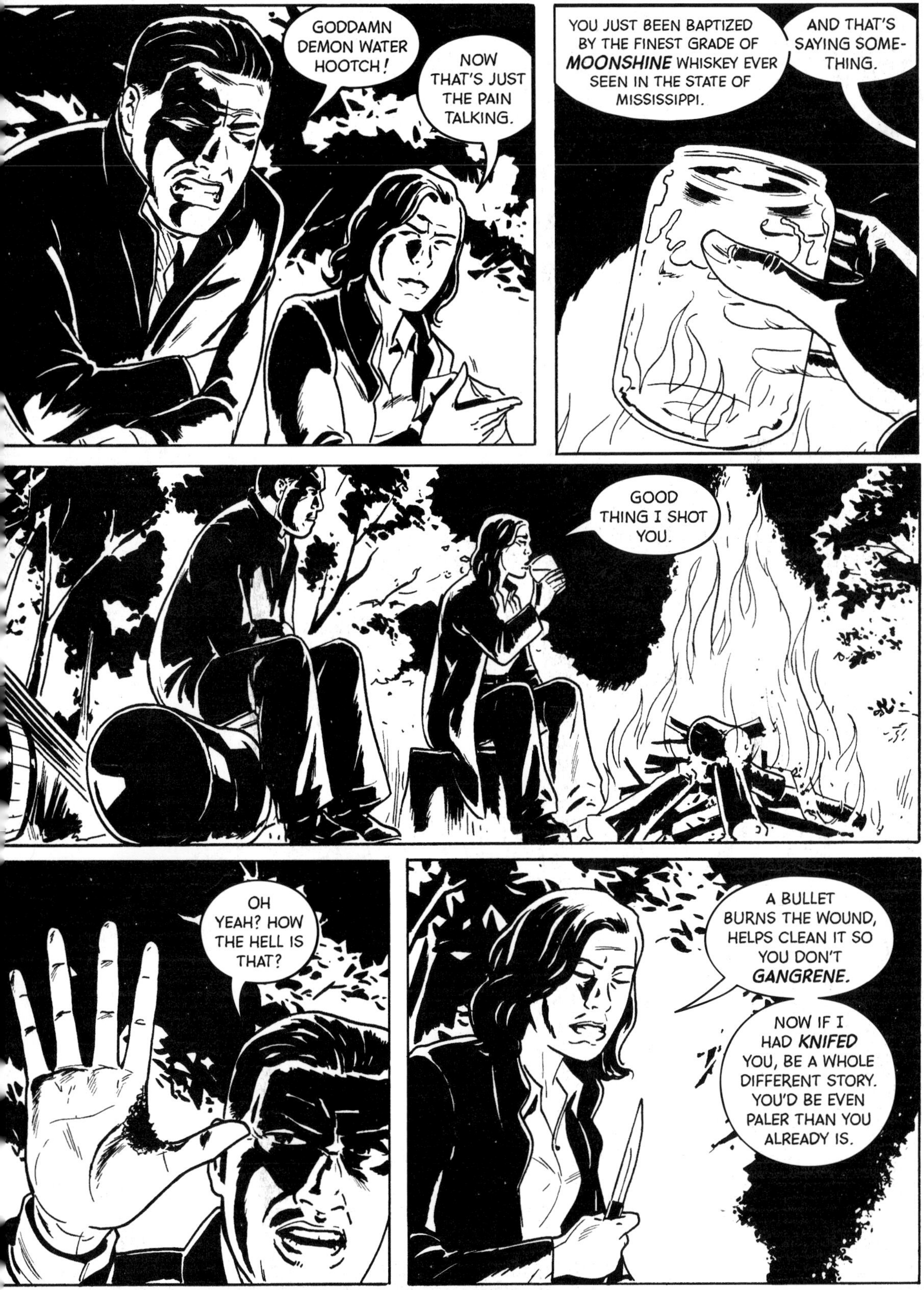
GODDAMN DEMON WATER HOOTCH!
NOW THAT'S JUST THE PAIN TALKING.
YOU JUST BEEN BAPTIZED BY THE FINEST GRADE OF **MOONSHINE** WHISKEY EVER SEEN IN THE STATE OF MISSISSIPPI.
AND THAT'S SAYING SOME-THING.
GOOD THING I SHOT YOU.
OH YEAH? HOW THE HELL IS THAT?
A BULLET BURNS THE WOUND, HELPS CLEAN IT SO YOU DON'T **GANGRENE.**
NOW IF I HAD **KNIFED** YOU, BE A WHOLE DIFFERENT STORY. YOU'D BE EVEN PALER THAN YOU ALREADY IS.

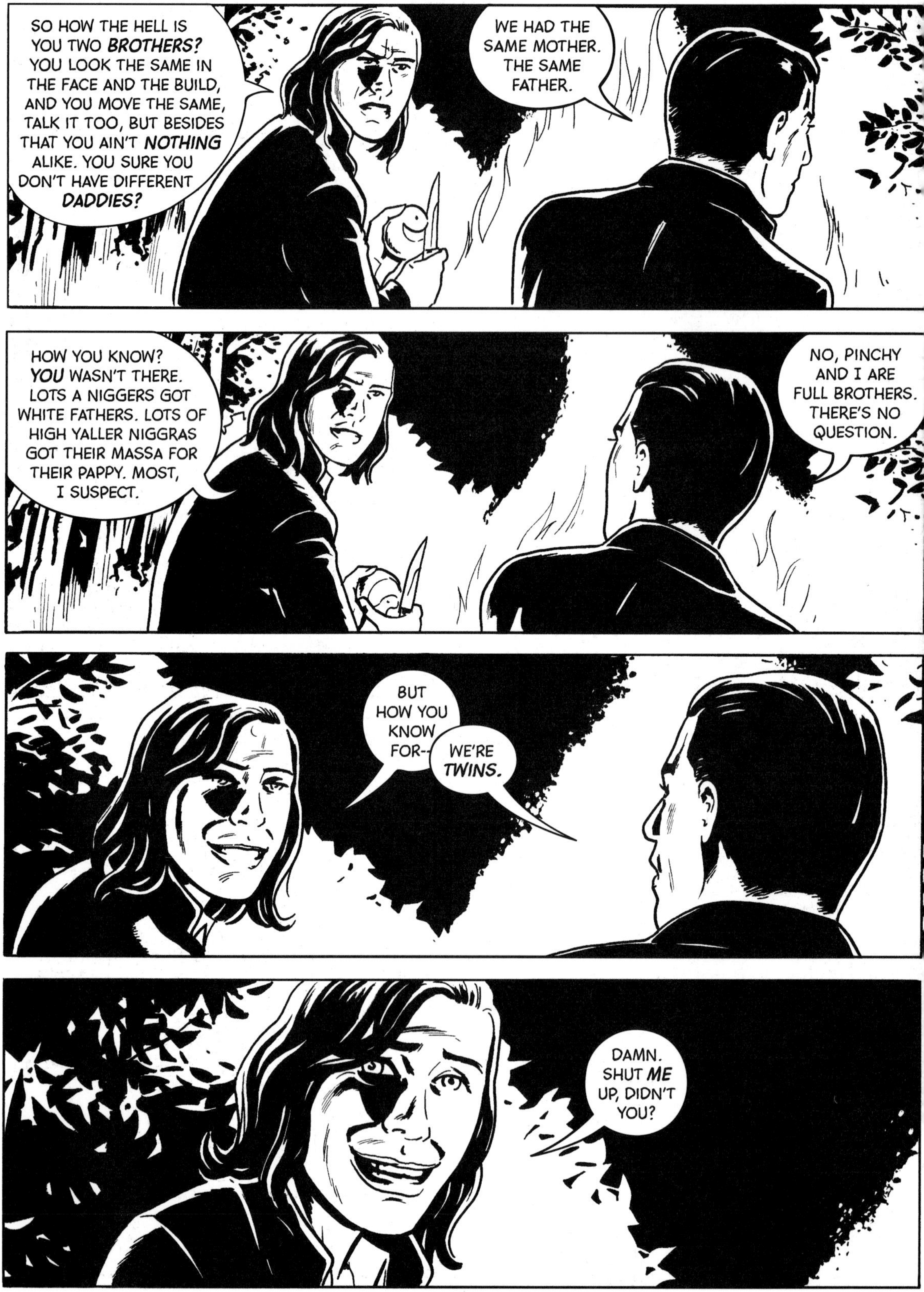
SO HOW THE HELL IS YOU TWO BROTHERS? YOU LOOK THE SAME IN THE FACE AND THE BUILD, AND YOU MOVE THE SAME, TALK IT TOO, BUT BESIDES THAT YOU AIN'T NOTHING ALIKE. YOU SURE YOU DON'T HAVE DIFFERENT DADDIES?
WE HAD THE SAME MOTHER. THE SAME FATHER.
HOW YOU KNOW? YOU WASN'T THERE. LOTS A NIGGERS GOT WHITE FATHERS. LOTS OF HIGH YALLER NIGGRAS GOT THEIR MASSA FOR THEIR PAPPY. MOST, I SUSPECT.
NO, PINCHY AND I ARE FULL BROTHERS. THERE'S NO QUESTION.
BUT HOW YOU KNOW FOR--
WE'RE TWINS.
DAMN. SHUT ME UP, DIDN'T YOU?

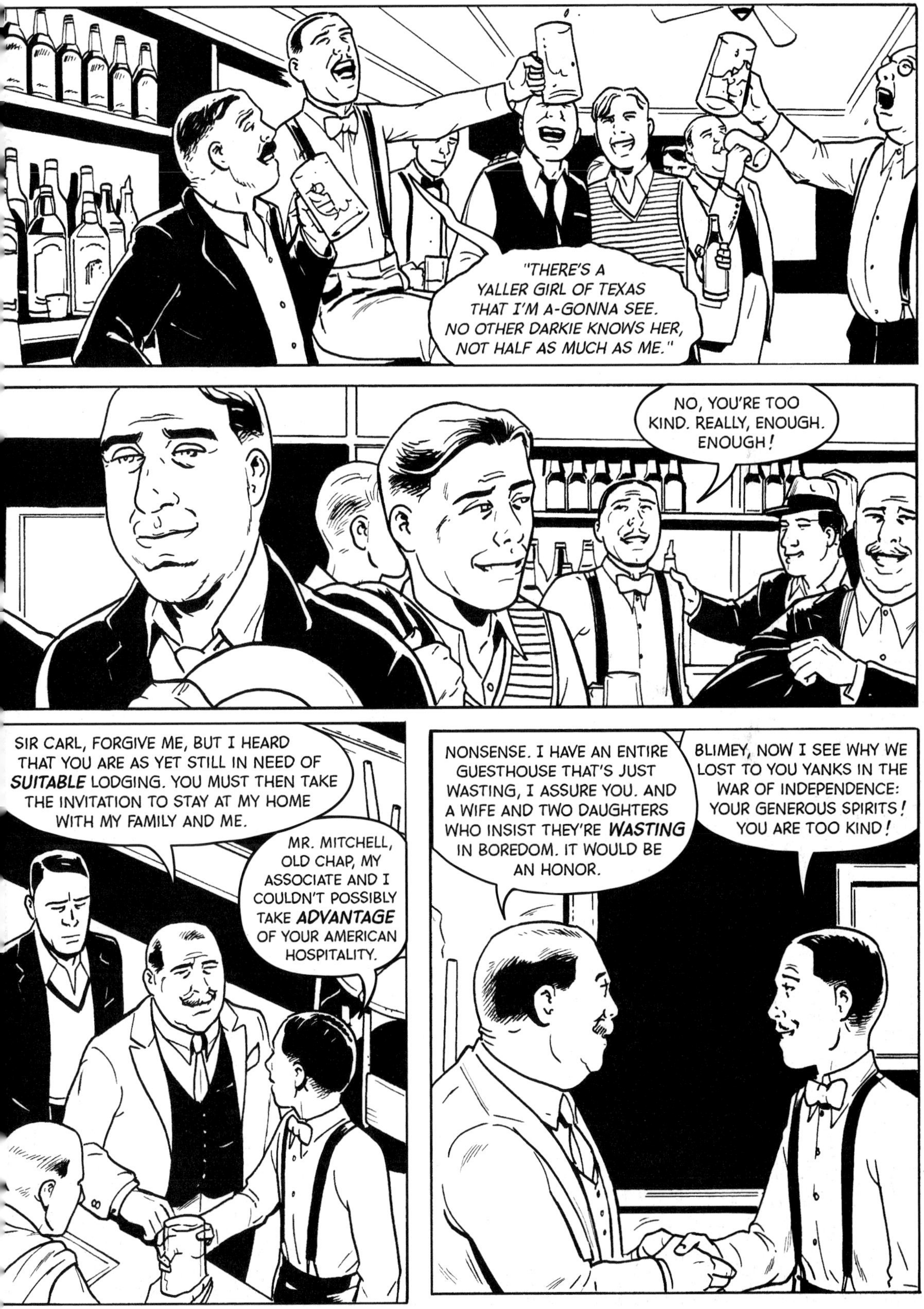
"THERE'S A YALLER GIRL OF TEXAS THAT I'M A-GONNA SEE. NO OTHER DARKIE KNOWS HER, NOT HALF AS MUCH AS ME."
NO, YOU'RE TOO KIND. REALLY, ENOUGH. ENOUGH!
SIR CARL, FORGIVE ME, BUT I HEARD THAT YOU ARE AS YET STILL IN NEED OF SUITABLE LODGING. YOU MUST THEN TAKE THE INVITATION TO STAY AT MY HOME WITH MY FAMILY AND ME.
MR. MITCHELL, OLD CHAP, MY ASSOCIATE AND I COULDN'T POSSIBLY TAKE ADVANTAGE OF YOUR AMERICAN HOSPITALITY.
NONSENSE. I HAVE AN ENTIRE GUESTHOUSE THAT'S JUST WASTING, I ASSURE YOU. AND A WIFE AND TWO DAUGHTERS WHO INSIST THEY'RE WASTING IN BOREDOM. IT WOULD BE AN HONOR.
BLIMEY, NOW I SEE WHY WE LOST TO YOU YANKS IN THE WAR OF INDEPENDENCE: YOUR GENEROUS SPIRITS! YOU ARE TOO KIND!

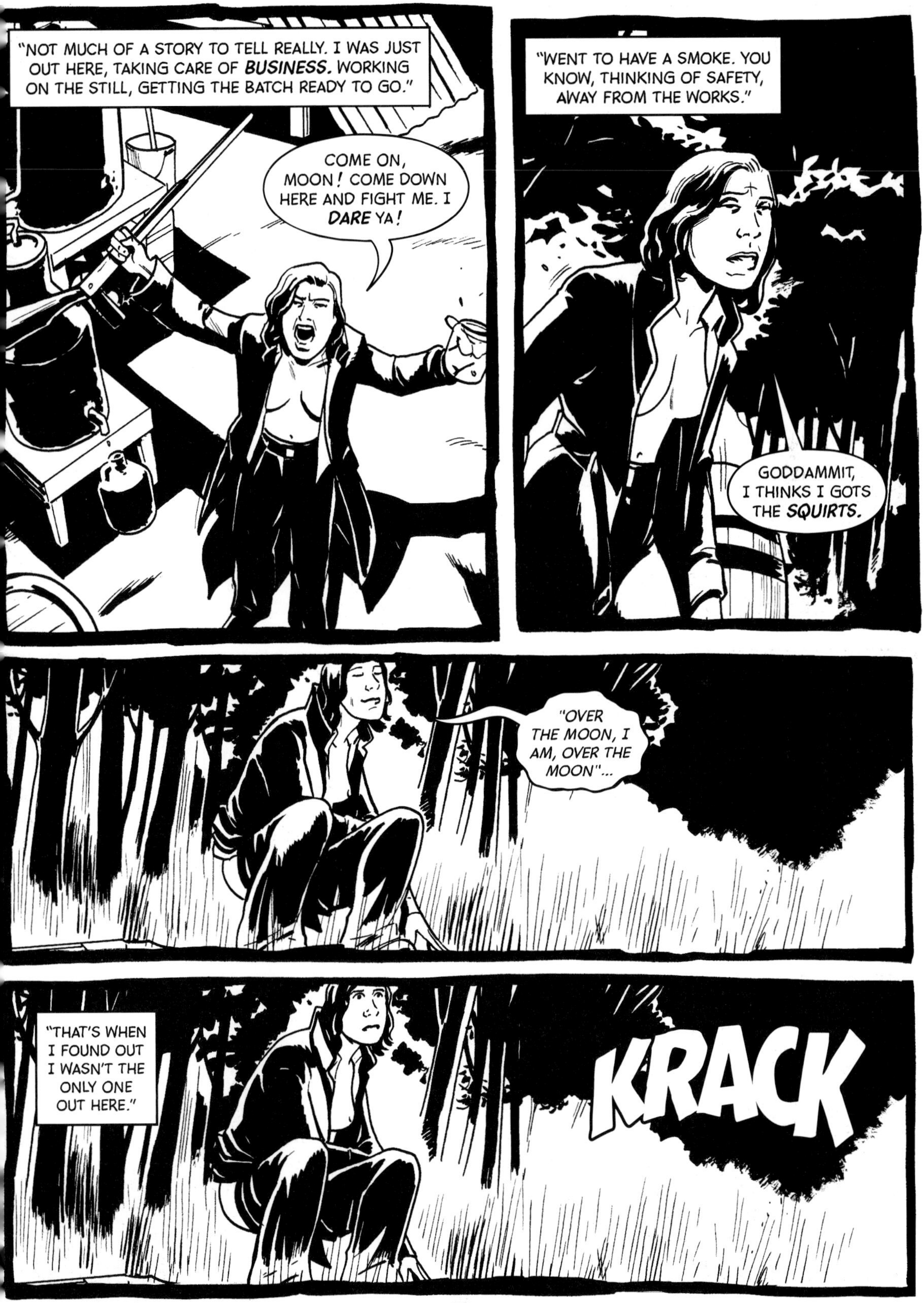
"NOT MUCH OF A STORY TO TELL REALLY. I WAS JUST OUT HERE, TAKING CARE OF BUSINESS. WORKING ON THE STILL, GETTING THE BATCH READY TO GO."
COME ON, MOON! COME DOWN HERE AND FIGHT ME. I DARE YA!
"WENT TO HAVE A SMOKE. YOU KNOW, THINKING OF SAFETY, AWAY FROM THE WORKS."
GODDAMMIT, I THINKS I GOTS THE SQUIRTS.
"OVER THE MOON, I AM, OVER THE MOON"...
"THAT'S WHEN I FOUND OUT I WASN'T THE ONLY ONE OUT HERE."
KRACK

SO THAT'S IT. I FOUND A GIRL'S BODY.

WHAT DO YOU MEAN, "THAT'S IT"? YOU JUST FOUND A GIRL'S BODY? THEN WHY DOES EVERYONE THINK THAT SHE WAS YOU?

"WELL, YOU KNOW, AT FIRST I WAS PRETTY SHOOK UP. I SEEN 'EM DEAD BEFORE, BUT STILL. SHE WAS ABOUT MY AGE, MY HEIGHT. GETS YOU THINKING.

"I LOOKED AT HER AND I THOUGHT, THE WAY I'M RUNNING, THIS IS HOW I'M GONNA END UP. MORE THAN ENOUGH PEOPLE WANT TO SEE ME DEAD, JUST LIKE THIS.

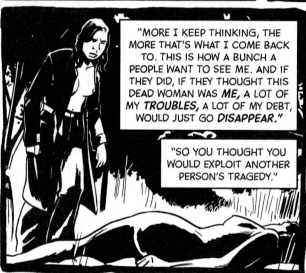

"MORE I KEEP THINKING, THE MORE THAT'S WHAT I COME BACK TO. THIS IS HOW A BUNCH A PEOPLE WANT TO SEE ME. AND IF THEY DID, IF THEY THOUGHT THIS DEAD WOMAN WAS ME, A LOT OF MY TROUBLES, A LOT OF MY DEBT, WOULD JUST GO DISAPPEAR."

"SO YOU THOUGHT YOU WOULD EXPLOIT ANOTHER PERSON'S TRAGEDY."

THERE ALREADY WAS A DEAD BODY THERE. IT SEEMED A SIN NOT TO USE IT.

SO I PUT MY CLOTHES ON HER.

"THEN I JUST GOT RID OF THOSE THINGS THAT MADE US DIFFERENT."

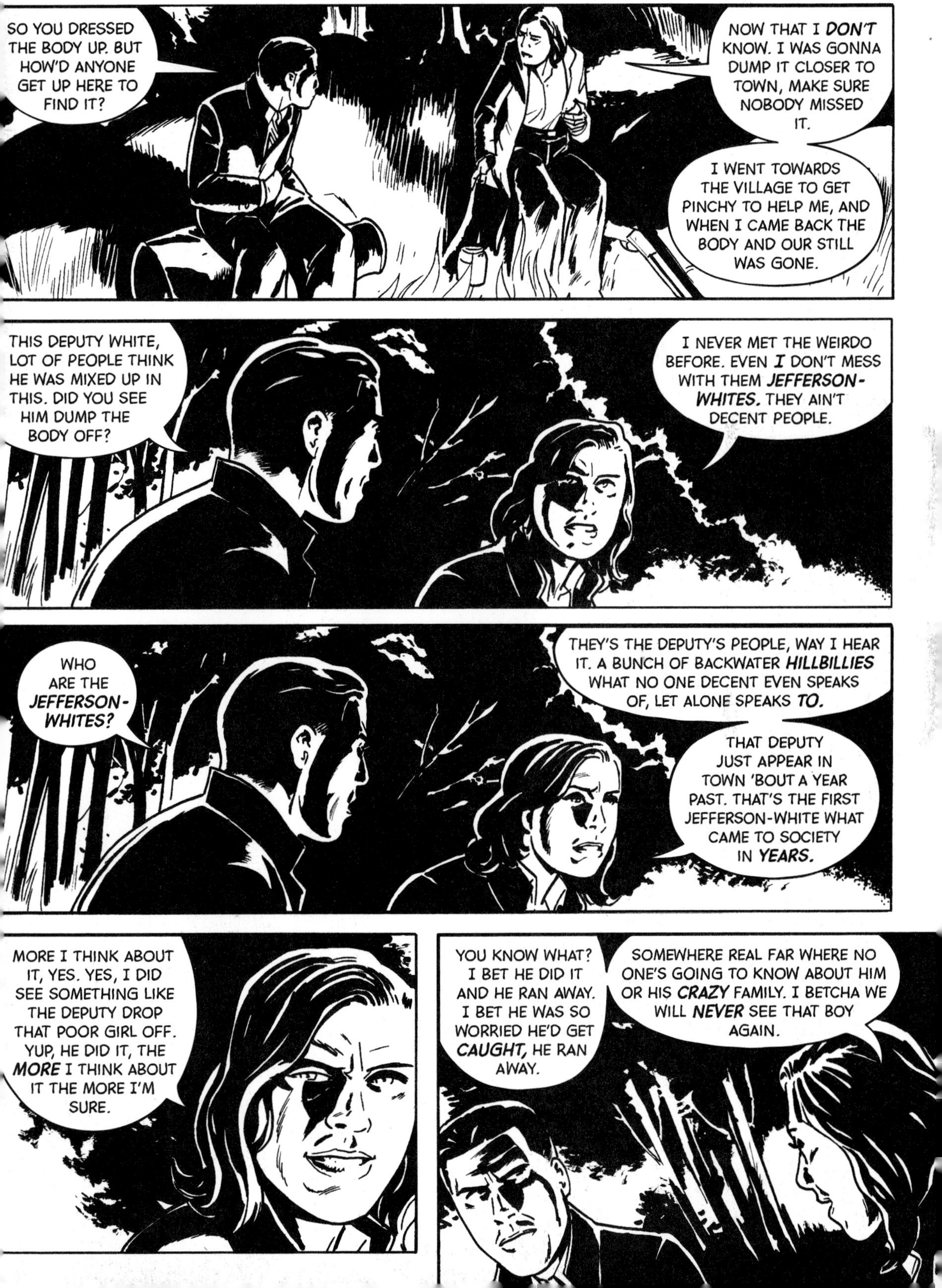
SO YOU DRESSED THE BODY UP. BUT HOW'D ANYONE GET UP HERE TO FIND IT?
NOW THAT I DON'T KNOW. I WAS GONNA DUMP IT CLOSER TO TOWN, MAKE SURE NOBODY MISSED IT.
I WENT TOWARDS THE VILLAGE TO GET PINCHY TO HELP ME, AND WHEN I CAME BACK THE BODY AND OUR STILL WAS GONE.
THIS DEPUTY WHITE, LOT OF PEOPLE THINK HE WAS MIXED UP IN THIS. DID YOU SEE HIM DUMP THE BODY OFF?
I NEVER MET THE WEIRDO BEFORE. EVEN I DON'T MESS WITH THEM JEFFERSON-WHITES. THEY AIN'T DECENT PEOPLE.
WHO ARE THE JEFFERSON-WHITES?
THEY'S THE DEPUTY'S PEOPLE, WAY I HEAR IT. A BUNCH OF BACKWATER HILLBILLIES WHAT NO ONE DECENT EVEN SPEAKS OF, LET ALONE SPEAKS TO.
THAT DEPUTY JUST APPEAR IN TOWN 'BOUT A YEAR PAST. THAT'S THE FIRST JEFFERSON-WHITE WHAT CAME TO SOCIETY IN YEARS.
MORE I THINK ABOUT IT, YES. YES, I DID SEE SOMETHING LIKE THE DEPUTY DROP THAT POOR GIRL OFF. YUP, HE DID IT, THE MORE I THINK ABOUT IT THE MORE I'M SURE.
YOU KNOW WHAT? I BET HE DID IT AND HE RAN AWAY. I BET HE WAS SO WORRIED HE'D GET CAUGHT, HE RAN AWAY.
SOMEWHERE REAL FAR WHERE NO ONE'S GOING TO KNOW ABOUT HIM OR HIS CRAZY FAMILY. I BETCHA WE WILL NEVER SEE THAT BOY AGAIN.

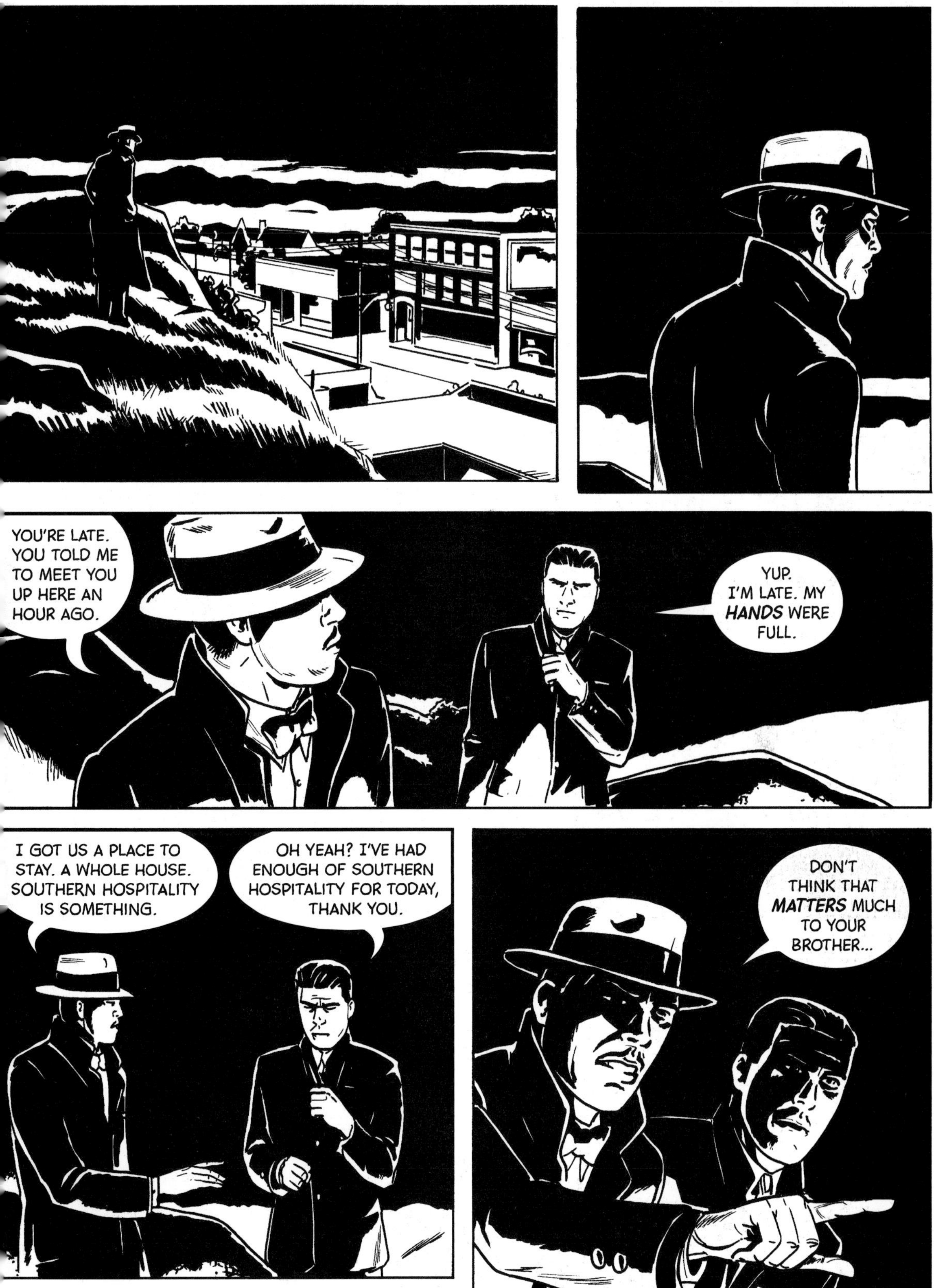
YOU'RE LATE. YOU TOLD ME TO MEET YOU UP HERE AN HOUR AGO.
YUP. I'M LATE. MY HANDS WERE FULL.
I GOT US A PLACE TO STAY. A WHOLE HOUSE. SOUTHERN HOSPITALITY IS SOMETHING.
OH YEAH? I'VE HAD ENOUGH OF SOUTHERN HOSPITALITY FOR TODAY, THANK YOU.
DON'T THINK THAT MATTERS MUCH TO YOUR BROTHER...

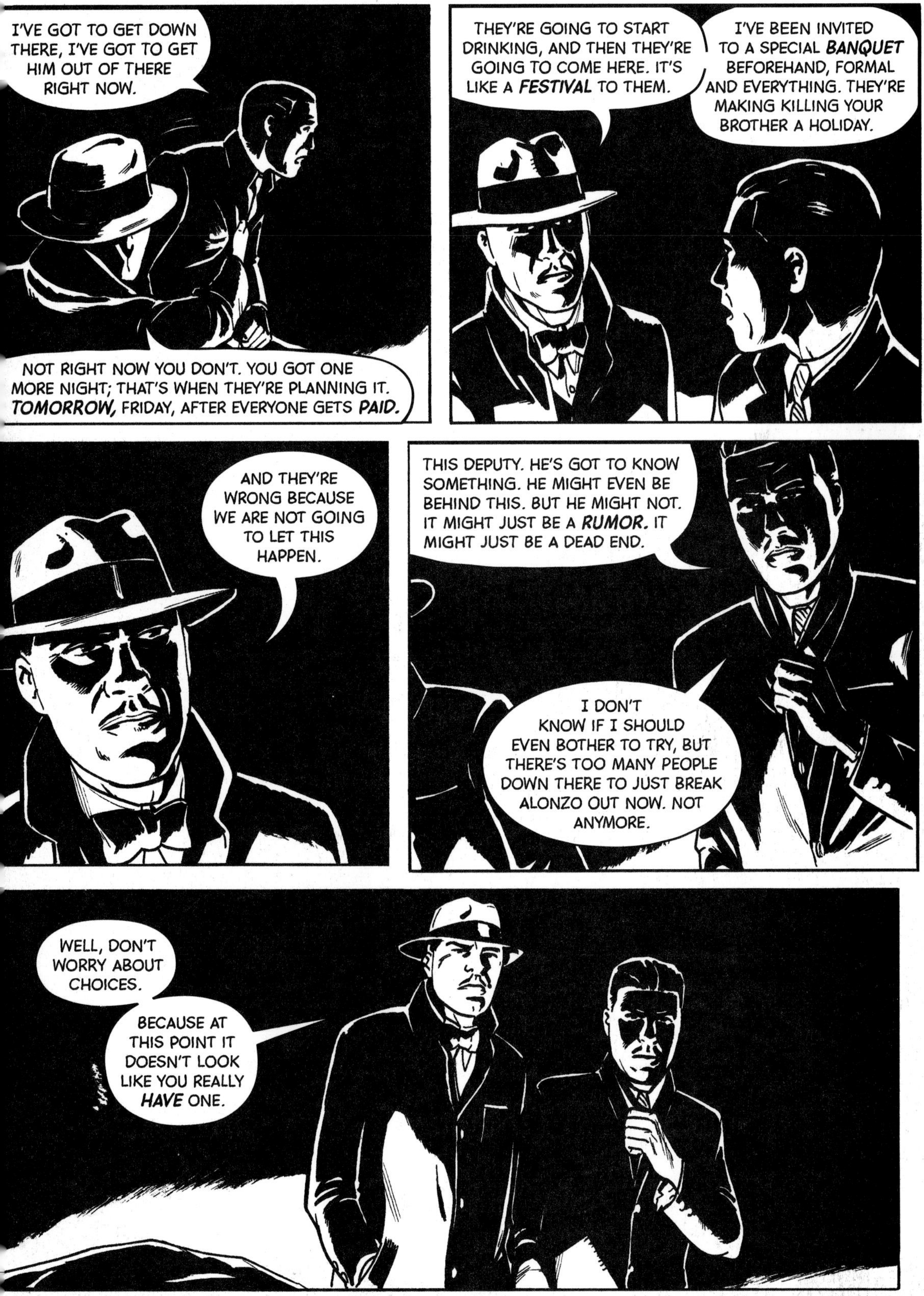

I'VE GOT TO GET DOWN THERE, I'VE GOT TO GET HIM OUT OF THERE RIGHT NOW.
NOT RIGHT NOW YOU DON'T. YOU GOT ONE MORE NIGHT; THAT'S WHEN THEY'RE PLANNING IT. **TOMORROW,** FRIDAY, AFTER EVERYONE GETS **PAID.**
THEY'RE GOING TO START DRINKING, AND THEN THEY'RE GOING TO COME HERE. IT'S LIKE A **FESTIVAL** TO THEM.
I'VE BEEN INVITED TO A SPECIAL **BANQUET** BEFOREHAND, FORMAL AND EVERYTHING. THEY'RE MAKING KILLING YOUR BROTHER A HOLIDAY.
AND THEY'RE WRONG BECAUSE WE ARE NOT GOING TO LET THIS HAPPEN.
THIS DEPUTY. HE'S GOT TO KNOW SOMETHING. HE MIGHT EVEN BE BEHIND THIS. BUT HE MIGHT NOT. IT MIGHT JUST BE A **RUMOR.** IT MIGHT JUST BE A DEAD END.
I DON'T KNOW IF I SHOULD EVEN BOTHER TO TRY, BUT THERE'S TOO MANY PEOPLE DOWN THERE TO JUST BREAK ALONZO OUT NOW. NOT ANYMORE.
WELL, DON'T WORRY ABOUT CHOICES.
BECAUSE AT THIS POINT IT DOESN'T LOOK LIKE YOU REALLY **HAVE** ONE.

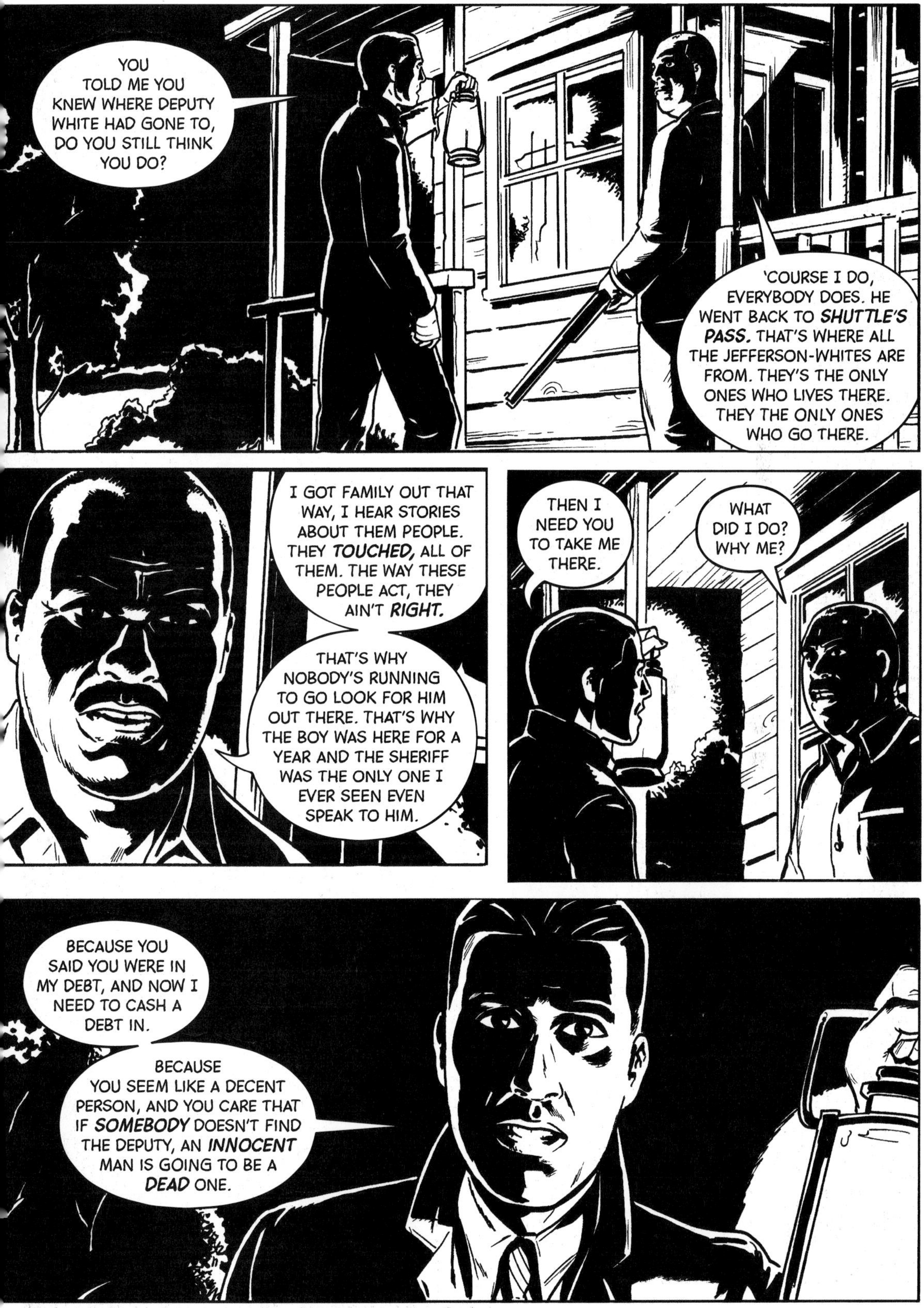
YOU TOLD ME YOU KNEW WHERE DEPUTY WHITE HAD GONE TO, DO YOU STILL THINK YOU DO?
'COURSE I DO, EVERYBODY DOES. HE WENT BACK TO SHUTTLE'S PASS. THAT'S WHERE ALL THE JEFFERSON-WHITES ARE FROM. THEY'S THE ONLY ONES WHO LIVES THERE. THEY THE ONLY ONES WHO GO THERE.
I GOT FAMILY OUT THAT WAY, I HEAR STORIES ABOUT THEM PEOPLE. THEY TOUCHED, ALL OF THEM. THE WAY THESE PEOPLE ACT, THEY AIN'T RIGHT.
THAT'S WHY NOBODY'S RUNNING TO GO LOOK FOR HIM OUT THERE. THAT'S WHY THE BOY WAS HERE FOR A YEAR AND THE SHERIFF WAS THE ONLY ONE I EVER SEEN EVEN SPEAK TO HIM.
THEN I NEED YOU TO TAKE ME THERE.
WHAT DID I DO? WHY ME?
BECAUSE YOU SAID YOU WERE IN MY DEBT, AND NOW I NEED TO CASH A DEBT IN.
BECAUSE YOU SEEM LIKE A DECENT PERSON, AND YOU CARE THAT IF SOMEBODY DOESN'T FIND THE DEPUTY, AN INNOCENT MAN IS GOING TO BE A DEAD ONE.

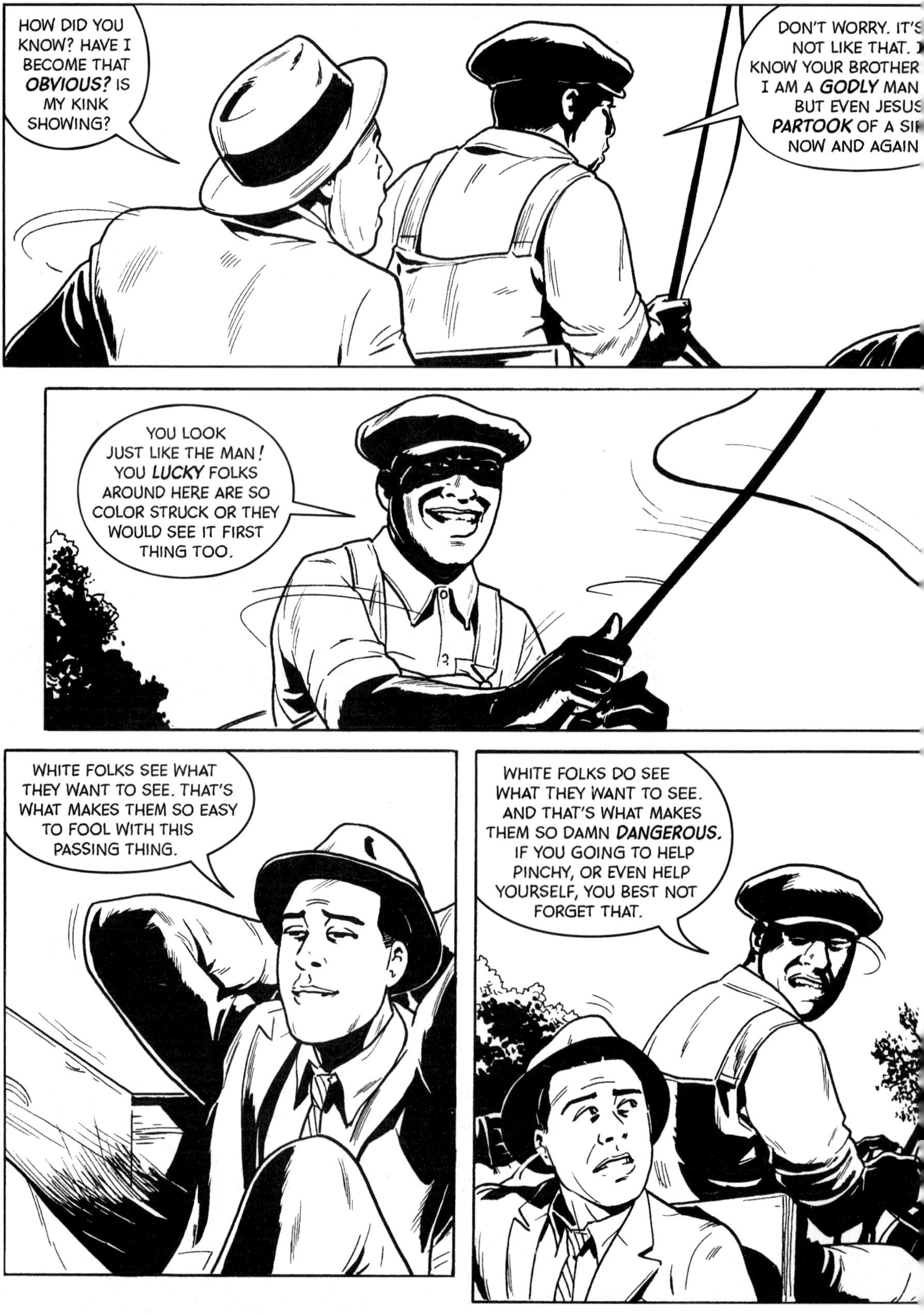
HOW DID YOU KNOW? HAVE I BECOME THAT OBVIOUS? IS MY KINK SHOWING?
DON'T WORRY. IT'S NOT LIKE THAT. I KNOW YOUR BROTHER I AM A GODLY MAN BUT EVEN JESUS PARTOOK OF A SI NOW AND AGAIN
YOU LOOK JUST LIKE THE MAN! YOU LUCKY FOLKS AROUND HERE ARE SO COLOR STRUCK OR THEY WOULD SEE IT FIRST THING TOO.
WHITE FOLKS SEE WHAT THEY WANT TO SEE. THAT'S WHAT MAKES THEM SO EASY TO FOOL WITH THIS PASSING THING.
WHITE FOLKS DO SEE WHAT THEY WANT TO SEE. AND THAT'S WHAT MAKES THEM SO DAMN DANGEROUS. IF YOU GOING TO HELP PINCHY, OR EVEN HELP YOURSELF, YOU BEST NOT FORGET THAT.

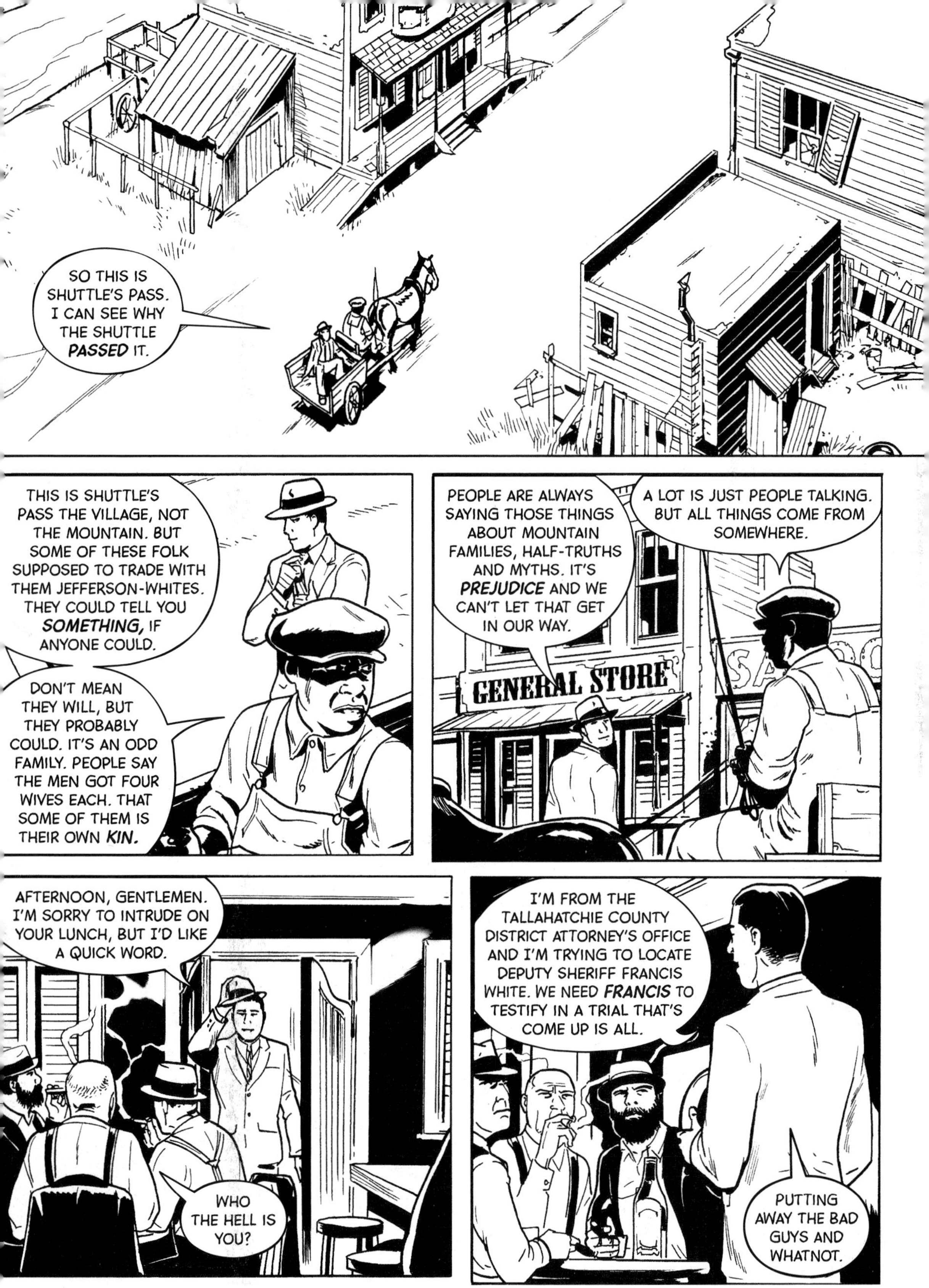
SO THIS IS SHUTTLE'S PASS. I CAN SEE WHY THE SHUTTLE PASSED IT.
THIS IS SHUTTLE'S PASS THE VILLAGE, NOT THE MOUNTAIN. BUT SOME OF THESE FOLK SUPPOSED TO TRADE WITH THEM JEFFERSON-WHITES. THEY COULD TELL YOU SOMETHING, IF ANYONE COULD.
DON'T MEAN THEY WILL, BUT THEY PROBABLY COULD. IT'S AN ODD FAMILY. PEOPLE SAY THE MEN GOT FOUR WIVES EACH. THAT SOME OF THEM IS THEIR OWN KIN.
PEOPLE ARE ALWAYS SAYING THOSE THINGS ABOUT MOUNTAIN FAMILIES, HALF-TRUTHS AND MYTHS. IT'S PREJUDICE AND WE CAN'T LET THAT GET IN OUR WAY.
A LOT IS JUST PEOPLE TALKING. BUT ALL THINGS COME FROM SOMEWHERE.
GENERAL STORE
AFTERNOON, GENTLEMEN. I'M SORRY TO INTRUDE ON YOUR LUNCH, BUT I'D LIKE A QUICK WORD.
WHO THE HELL IS YOU?
I'M FROM THE TALLAHATCHIE COUNTY DISTRICT ATTORNEY'S OFFICE AND I'M TRYING TO LOCATE DEPUTY SHERIFF FRANCIS WHITE. WE NEED FRANCIS TO TESTIFY IN A TRIAL THAT'S COME UP IS ALL.
PUTTING AWAY THE BAD GUYS AND WHATNOT.

PART II

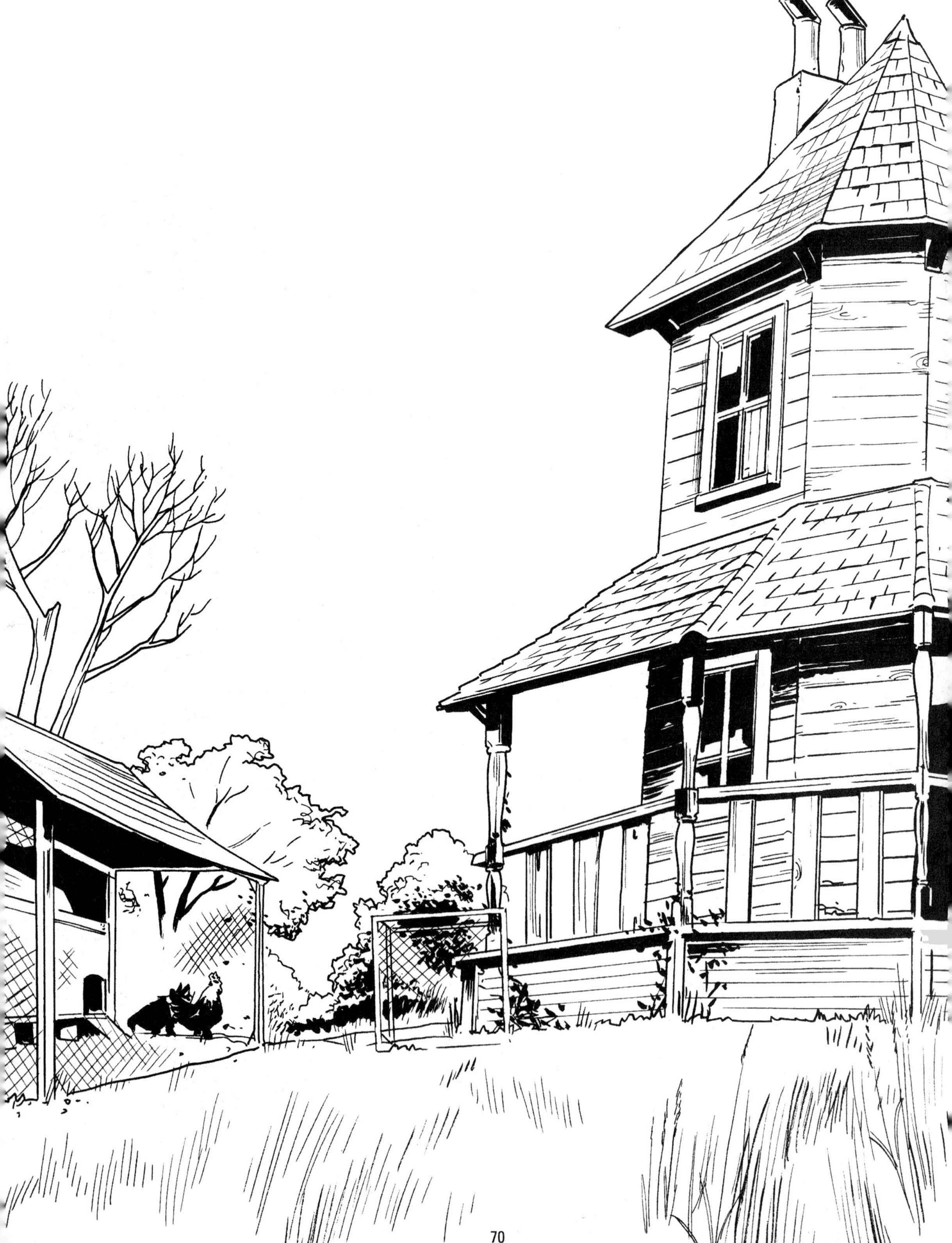

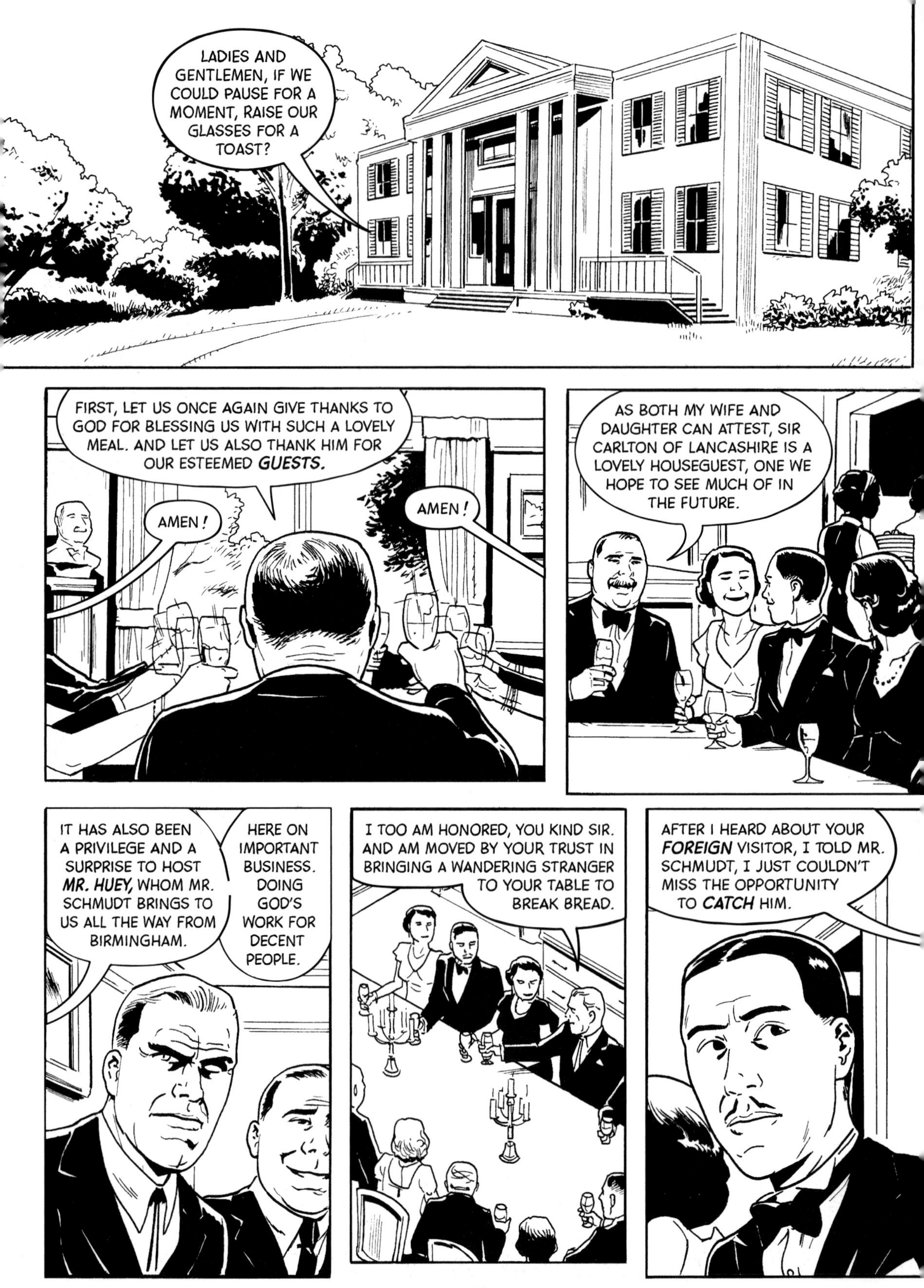
LADIES AND GENTLEMEN, IF WE COULD PAUSE FOR A MOMENT, RAISE OUR GLASSES FOR A TOAST?
FIRST, LET US ONCE AGAIN GIVE THANKS TO GOD FOR BLESSING US WITH SUCH A LOVELY MEAL. AND LET US ALSO THANK HIM FOR OUR ESTEEMED GUESTS.
AMEN!
AMEN!
AS BOTH MY WIFE AND DAUGHTER CAN ATTEST, SIR CARLTON OF LANCASHIRE IS A LOVELY HOUSEGUEST, ONE WE HOPE TO SEE MUCH OF IN THE FUTURE.
IT HAS ALSO BEEN A PRIVILEGE AND A SURPRISE TO HOST MR. HUEY, WHOM MR. SCHMUDT BRINGS TO US ALL THE WAY FROM BIRMINGHAM.
HERE ON IMPORTANT BUSINESS. DOING GOD'S WORK FOR DECENT PEOPLE.
I TOO AM HONORED, YOU KIND SIR. AND AM MOVED BY YOUR TRUST IN BRINGING A WANDERING STRANGER TO YOUR TABLE TO BREAK BREAD.
AFTER I HEARD ABOUT YOUR FOREIGN VISITOR, I TOLD MR. SCHMUDT, I JUST COULDN'T MISS THE OPPORTUNITY TO CATCH HIM.

YOU TALK FUNNY. DON'T YA?

I WOULDN'T SAY I TALK FUNNY, PEOPLE FROM DIFFERENT PLACES TALK IN DIFFERENT WAYS.

SO YOU SAYING *EVERYBODY* WHERE YOU FROM TALK FUNNY LIKE YOU? THAT'S CRAZY.

YOU SOUND LIKE THE BUTLER ON *THE EDDIE CANTOR RADIO SHOW.*

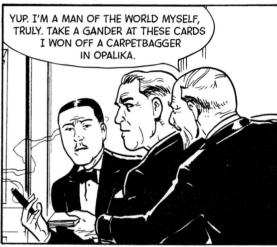

YUP. I'M A MAN OF THE WORLD MYSELF, TRULY. TAKE A GANDER AT THESE CARDS I WON OFF A CARPETBAGGER IN OPALIKA.

THE QUEEN OF HEARTS, SHE'S MY FAVORITE. YOU CAN EVEN SEE WHERE THE BABIES COME OUT.

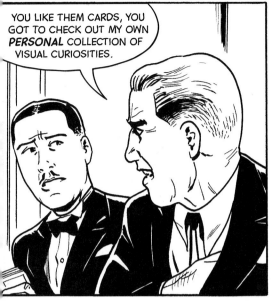

YOU LIKE THEM CARDS, YOU GOT TO CHECK OUT MY OWN *PERSONAL* COLLECTION OF VISUAL CURIOSITIES.

WELL I'LL BE, THAT NIGGER'S NECK IS SNAPPED JUST LIKE A TURKEY'S. THEY ROASTED HIM THE SAME, TOO.

NOW WILL YOU LOOK AT THAT, NOW THAT IS QUITE A COLLECTION. YOU BUY THEM AS A GROUP?

OH NO. I BOUGHT EACH AND EVERY ONE RIGHT THERE THE DAY THEY WERE MADE. YOU COULD STILL SMELL THE *MEAT* IN THE AIR.

HEY, WILL YOU LOOK AT THIS ONE, YOU GOT ONE OF A *WHITE* MAN GETTING THE GIBBET TOO.

OH NO, HE'S A NIGGER ALL RIGHT. HE *LOOKED* LIKE A WHITE MAN, BUT HE WAS JUST A NIGGER TRYING TO *PASS.*

HOW DID YOU KNOW FOR CERTAIN?

DON'T YOU WORRY. IF THERE'S ONE THING I KNOWS IT'S NIGGERS, AND I KNOW A NIGGER WHEN I SEE ONE. NO MATTER HOW *PALE* HIS SKIN MIGHT BE.

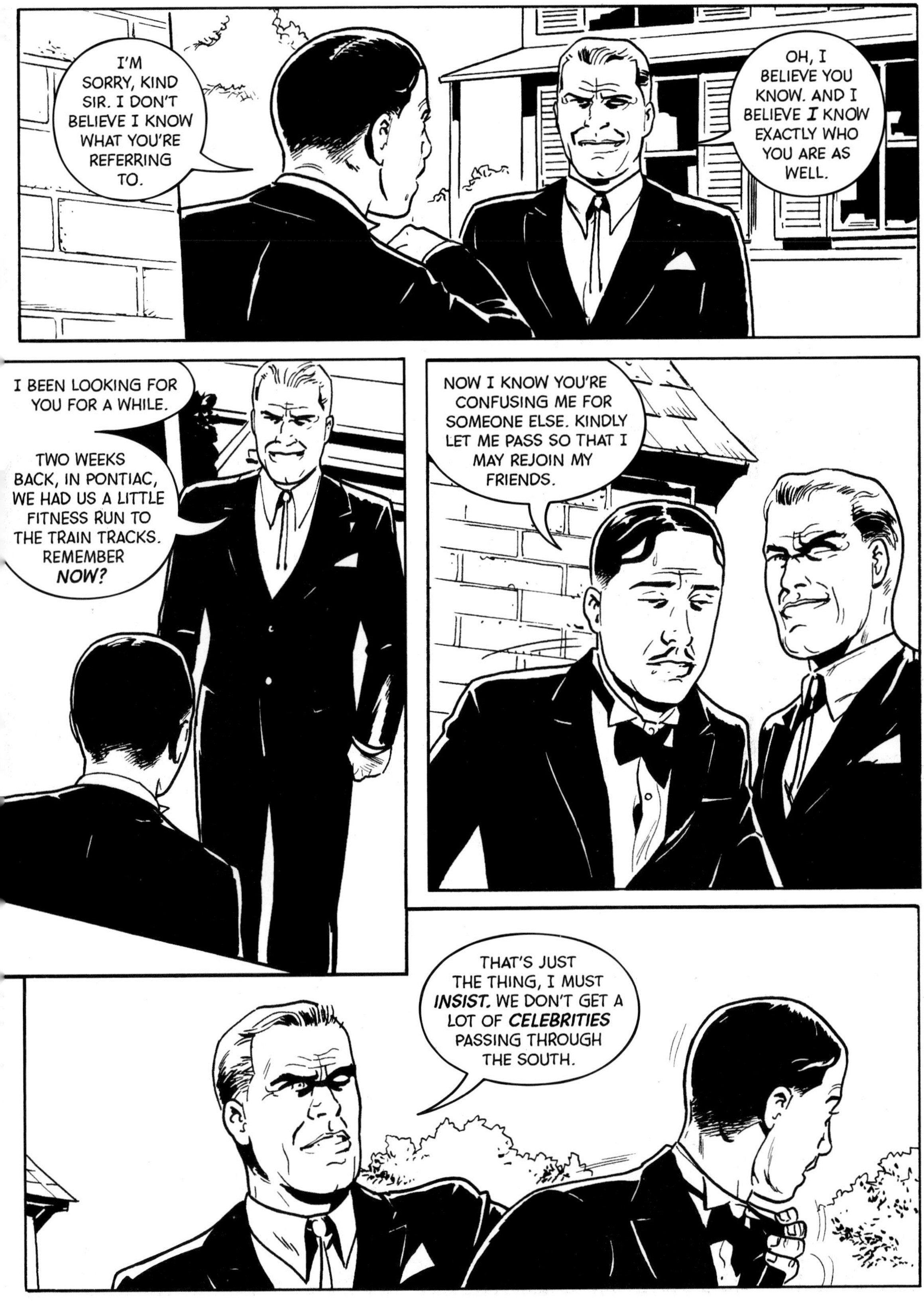
I'M SORRY, KIND SIR. I DON'T BELIEVE I KNOW WHAT YOU'RE REFERRING TO.
OH, I BELIEVE YOU KNOW. AND I BELIEVE *I* KNOW EXACTLY WHO YOU ARE AS WELL.
I BEEN LOOKING FOR YOU FOR A WHILE.
TWO WEEKS BACK, IN PONTIAC, WE HAD US A LITTLE FITNESS RUN TO THE TRAIN TRACKS. REMEMBER *NOW?*
NOW I KNOW YOU'RE CONFUSING ME FOR SOMEONE ELSE. KINDLY LET ME PASS SO THAT I MAY REJOIN MY FRIENDS.
THAT'S JUST THE THING, I MUST *INSIST.* WE DON'T GET A LOT OF *CELEBRITIES* PASSING THROUGH THE SOUTH.

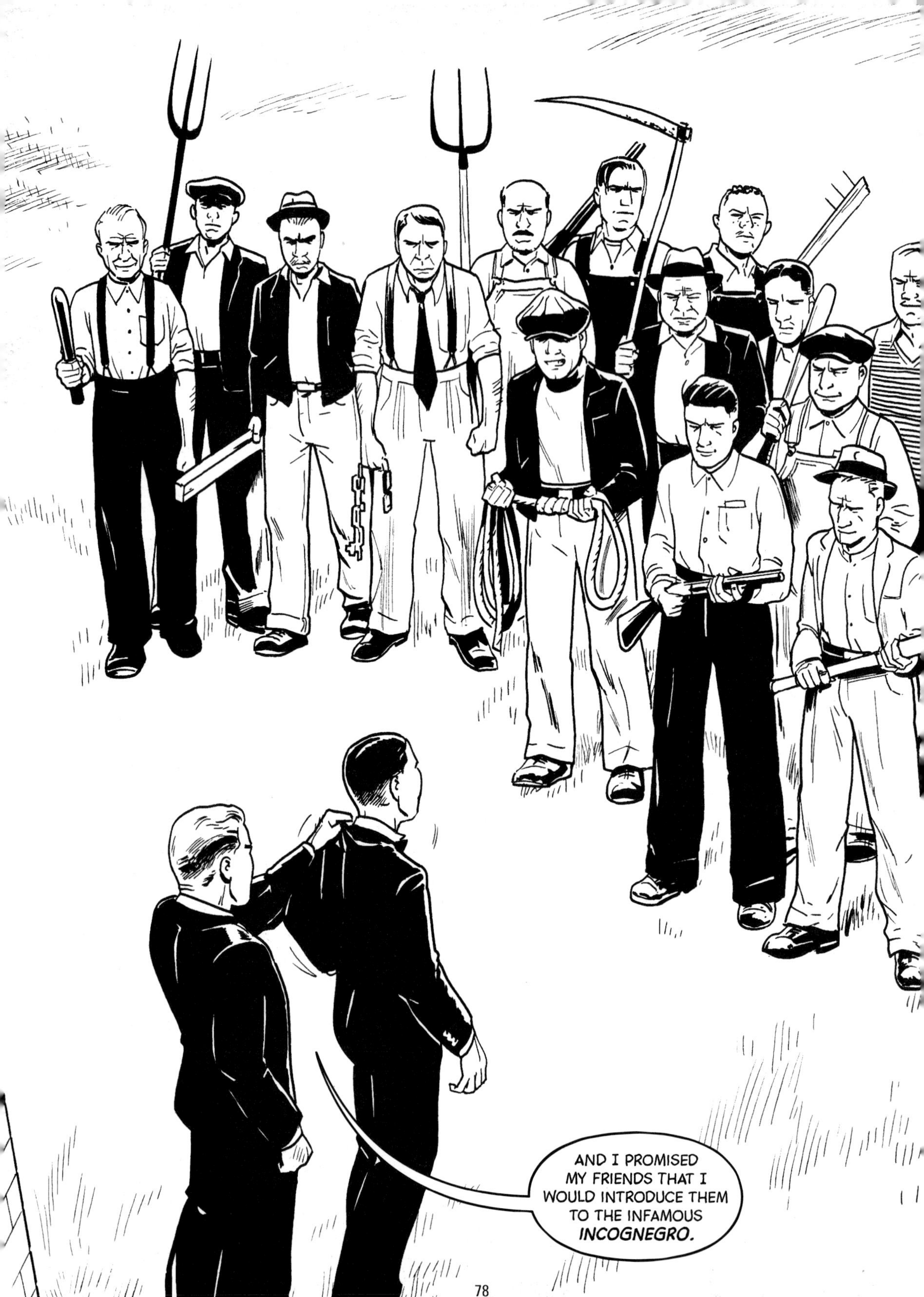
AND I PROMISED MY FRIENDS THAT I WOULD INTRODUCE THEM TO THE INFAMOUS ***INCOGNEGRO.***

WAKES UP!

MY OLD MAN SAY, WAKES UP! IS THE NIGGERS *RISING?*

COME ON, *SAY* SOMETHING.

I KNOW'D AS SOON AS ELMER DRAGGED YOU IN HERE. THE NIGGERS IS *RISING,* AIN'T THEY? JUST LIKE I BEEN SAYING, AND MY PA BEFORE ME. THE NIGGERS IS FINALLY RISING, THE DAY IS HERE.

WHAT? LOOK, THERE SEEMS TO BE SOME--

WE TOLD 'EM. WE SAID, YOU CAN ONLY BEAT A DOG FOR SO LONG. THEY GOING TO RISE UP, SLAY YOU. JUST LIKE THEY DONE THE PHARAOHS OF OLD.

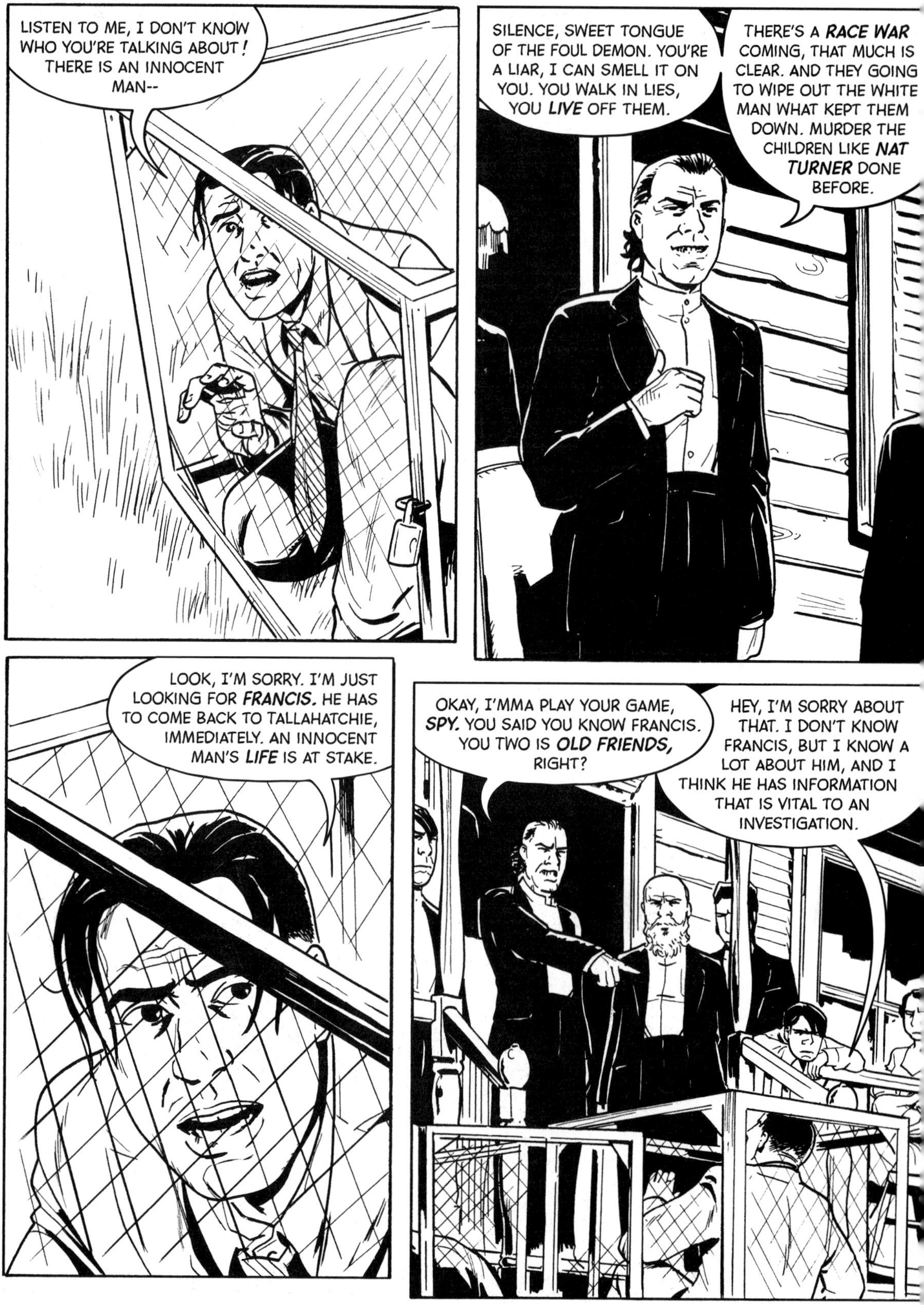

LISTEN TO ME, I DON'T KNOW WHO YOU'RE TALKING ABOUT! THERE IS AN INNOCENT MAN--
SILENCE, SWEET TONGUE OF THE FOUL DEMON. YOU'RE A LIAR, I CAN SMELL IT ON YOU. YOU WALK IN LIES, YOU LIVE OFF THEM.
THERE'S A RACE WAR COMING, THAT MUCH IS CLEAR. AND THEY GOING TO WIPE OUT THE WHITE MAN WHAT KEPT THEM DOWN. MURDER THE CHILDREN LIKE NAT TURNER DONE BEFORE.
LOOK, I'M SORRY. I'M JUST LOOKING FOR FRANCIS. HE HAS TO COME BACK TO TALLAHATCHIE, IMMEDIATELY. AN INNOCENT MAN'S LIFE IS AT STAKE.
OKAY, I'MMA PLAY YOUR GAME, SPY. YOU SAID YOU KNOW FRANCIS. YOU TWO IS OLD FRIENDS, RIGHT?
HEY, I'M SORRY ABOUT THAT. I DON'T KNOW FRANCIS, BUT I KNOW A LOT ABOUT HIM, AND I THINK HE HAS INFORMATION THAT IS VITAL TO AN INVESTIGATION.

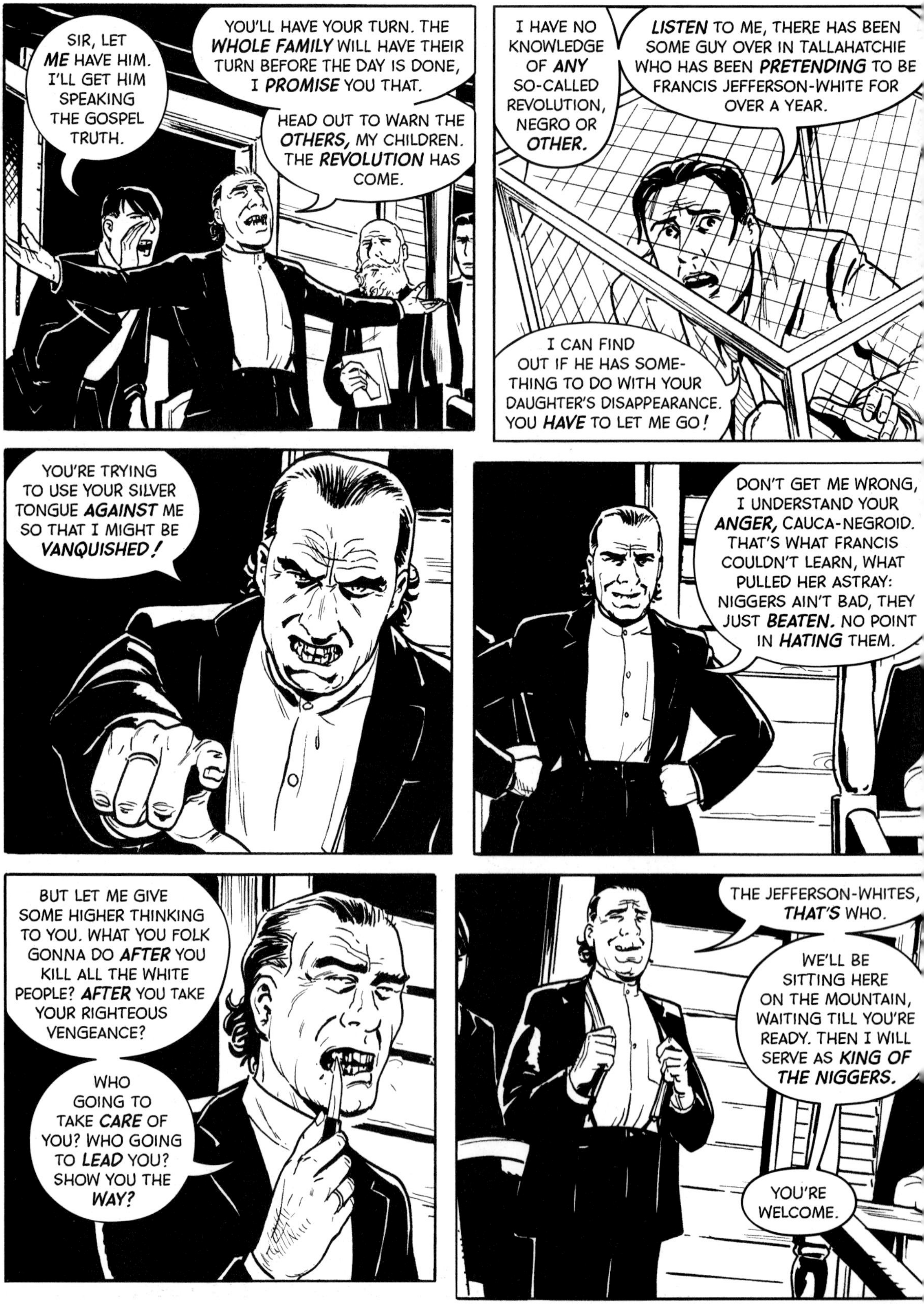
SIR, LET ME HAVE HIM. I'LL GET HIM SPEAKING THE GOSPEL TRUTH.
YOU'LL HAVE YOUR TURN. THE WHOLE FAMILY WILL HAVE THEIR TURN BEFORE THE DAY IS DONE, I PROMISE YOU THAT.
HEAD OUT TO WARN THE OTHERS, MY CHILDREN. THE REVOLUTION HAS COME.
I HAVE NO KNOWLEDGE OF ANY SO-CALLED REVOLUTION, NEGRO OR OTHER.
LISTEN TO ME, THERE HAS BEEN SOME GUY OVER IN TALLAHATCHIE WHO HAS BEEN PRETENDING TO BE FRANCIS JEFFERSON-WHITE FOR OVER A YEAR.
I CAN FIND OUT IF HE HAS SOMETHING TO DO WITH YOUR DAUGHTER'S DISAPPEARANCE. YOU HAVE TO LET ME GO!
YOU'RE TRYING TO USE YOUR SILVER TONGUE AGAINST ME SO THAT I MIGHT BE VANQUISHED!
DON'T GET ME WRONG, I UNDERSTAND YOUR ANGER, CAUCA-NEGROID. THAT'S WHAT FRANCIS COULDN'T LEARN, WHAT PULLED HER ASTRAY: NIGGERS AIN'T BAD, THEY JUST BEATEN. NO POINT IN HATING THEM.
BUT LET ME GIVE SOME HIGHER THINKING TO YOU. WHAT YOU FOLK GONNA DO AFTER YOU KILL ALL THE WHITE PEOPLE? AFTER YOU TAKE YOUR RIGHTEOUS VENGEANCE?
WHO GOING TO TAKE CARE OF YOU? WHO GOING TO LEAD YOU? SHOW YOU THE WAY?
THE JEFFERSON-WHITES, THAT'S WHO.
WE'LL BE SITTING HERE ON THE MOUNTAIN, WAITING TILL YOU'RE READY. THEN I WILL SERVE AS KING OF THE NIGGERS.
YOU'RE WELCOME.

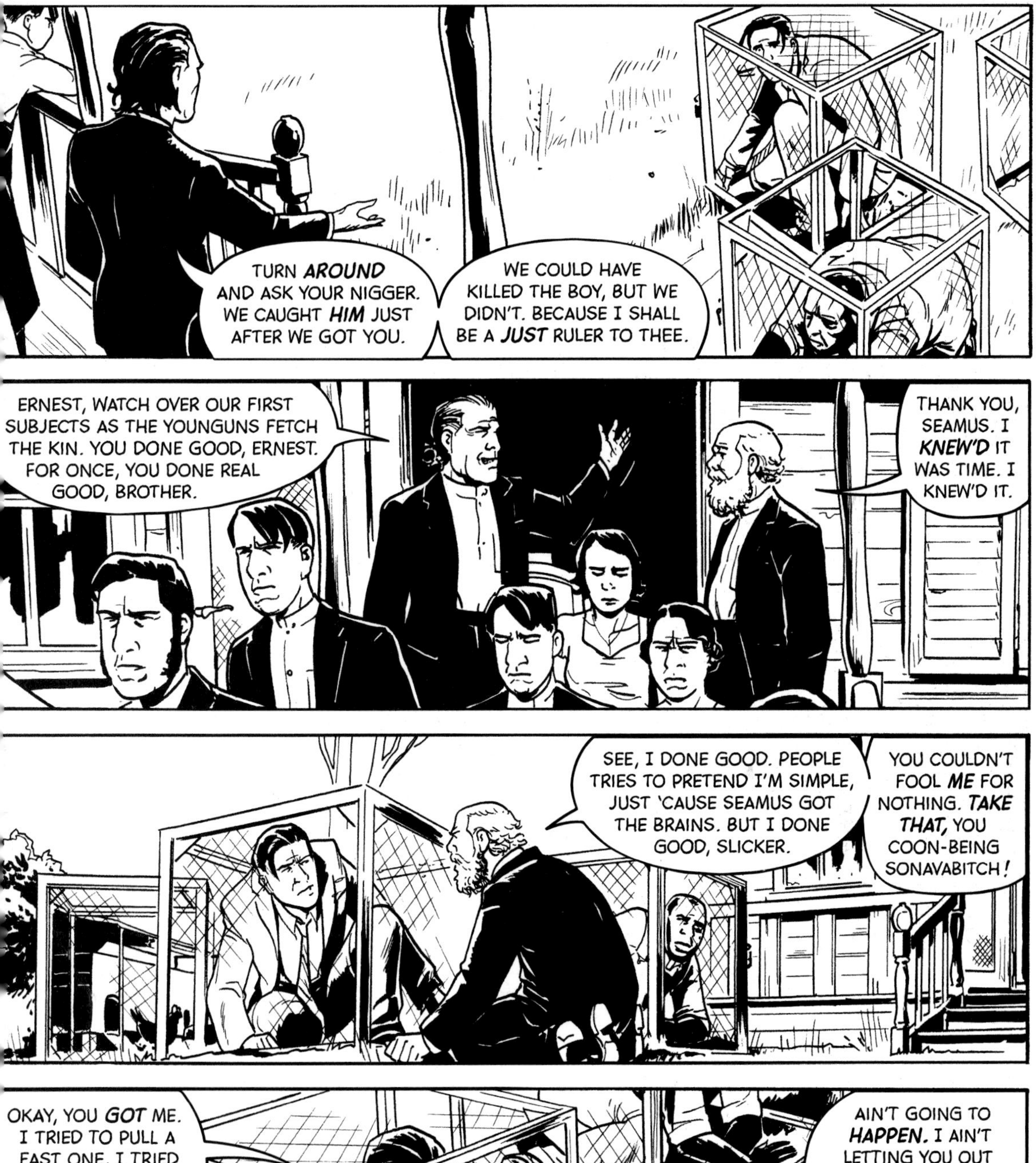
TURN AROUND AND ASK YOUR NIGGER. WE CAUGHT HIM JUST AFTER WE GOT YOU.
WE COULD HAVE KILLED THE BOY, BUT WE DIDN'T. BECAUSE I SHALL BE A JUST RULER TO THEE.
ERNEST, WATCH OVER OUR FIRST SUBJECTS AS THE YOUNGUNS FETCH THE KIN. YOU DONE GOOD, ERNEST. FOR ONCE, YOU DONE REAL GOOD, BROTHER.
THANK YOU, SEAMUS. I KNEW'D IT WAS TIME. I KNEW'D IT.
SEE, I DONE GOOD. PEOPLE TRIES TO PRETEND I'M SIMPLE, JUST 'CAUSE SEAMUS GOT THE BRAINS. BUT I DONE GOOD, SLICKER.
YOU COULDN'T FOOL ME FOR NOTHING. TAKE THAT, YOU COON-BEING SONAVABITCH!
OKAY, YOU GOT ME. I TRIED TO PULL A FAST ONE, I TRIED TO BE SLICK, AND YOU GOT ME, OKAY? JUST LET ME GO!
AIN'T GOING TO HAPPEN. I AIN'T LETTING YOU OUT SO YOU CAN WARN YOUR BRETHREN. Y'ALL DON'T KNOW WHAT'S GOOD FOR YOU.

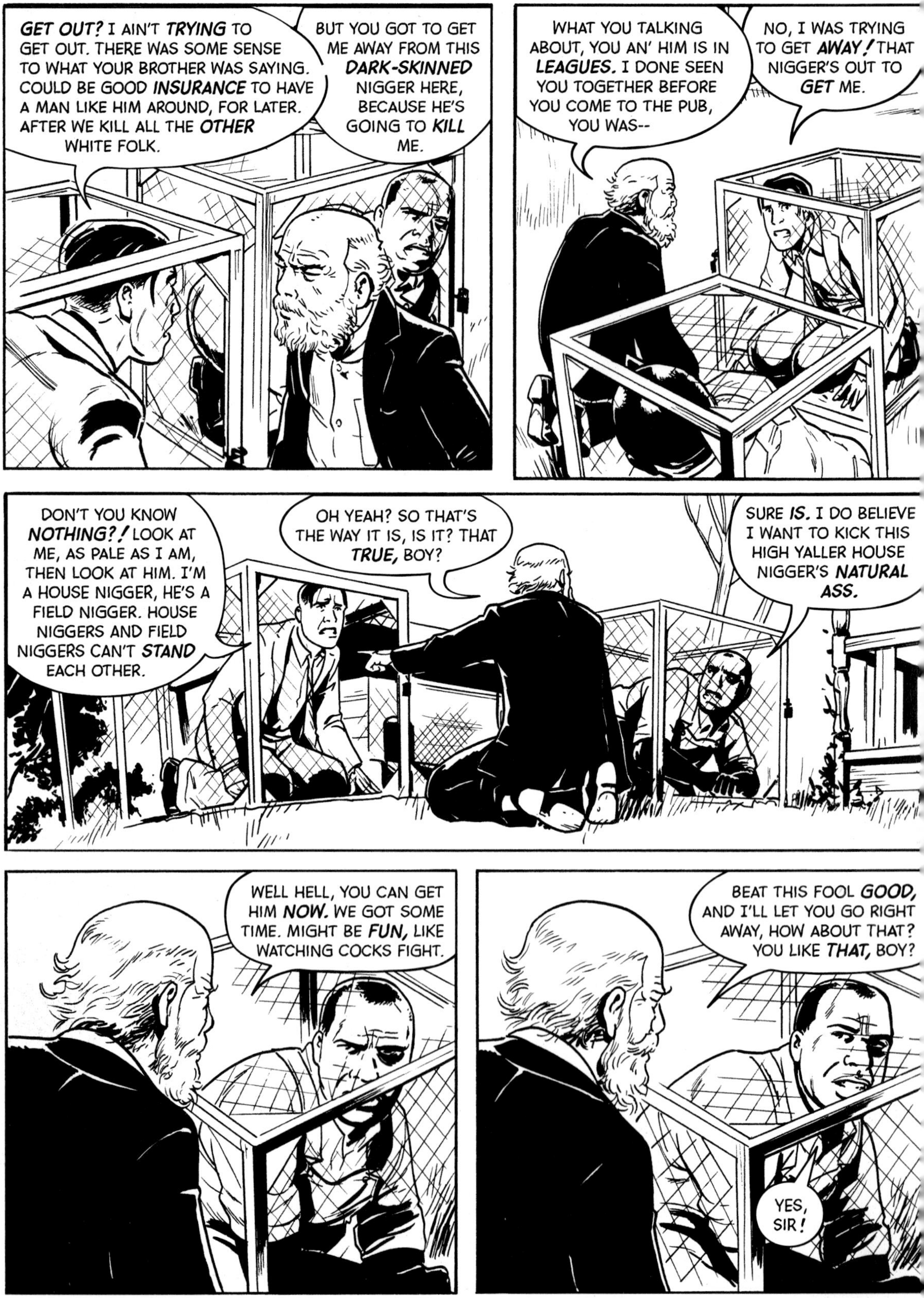
GET OUT? I AIN'T TRYING TO GET OUT. THERE WAS SOME SENSE TO WHAT YOUR BROTHER WAS SAYING. COULD BE GOOD INSURANCE TO HAVE A MAN LIKE HIM AROUND, FOR LATER. AFTER WE KILL ALL THE OTHER WHITE FOLK.
BUT YOU GOT TO GET ME AWAY FROM THIS DARK-SKINNED NIGGER HERE, BECAUSE HE'S GOING TO KILL ME.
WHAT YOU TALKING ABOUT, YOU AN' HIM IS IN LEAGUES. I DONE SEEN YOU TOGETHER BEFORE YOU COME TO THE PUB, YOU WAS--
NO, I WAS TRYING TO GET AWAY! THAT NIGGER'S OUT TO GET ME.
DON'T YOU KNOW NOTHING?! LOOK AT ME, AS PALE AS I AM, THEN LOOK AT HIM. I'M A HOUSE NIGGER, HE'S A FIELD NIGGER. HOUSE NIGGERS AND FIELD NIGGERS CAN'T STAND EACH OTHER.
OH YEAH? SO THAT'S THE WAY IT IS, IS IT? THAT TRUE, BOY?
SURE IS. I DO BELIEVE I WANT TO KICK THIS HIGH YALLER HOUSE NIGGER'S NATURAL ASS.
WELL HELL, YOU CAN GET HIM NOW. WE GOT SOME TIME. MIGHT BE FUN, LIKE WATCHING COCKS FIGHT.
BEAT THIS FOOL GOOD, AND I'LL LET YOU GO RIGHT AWAY, HOW ABOUT THAT? YOU LIKE THAT, BOY?
YES, SIR!

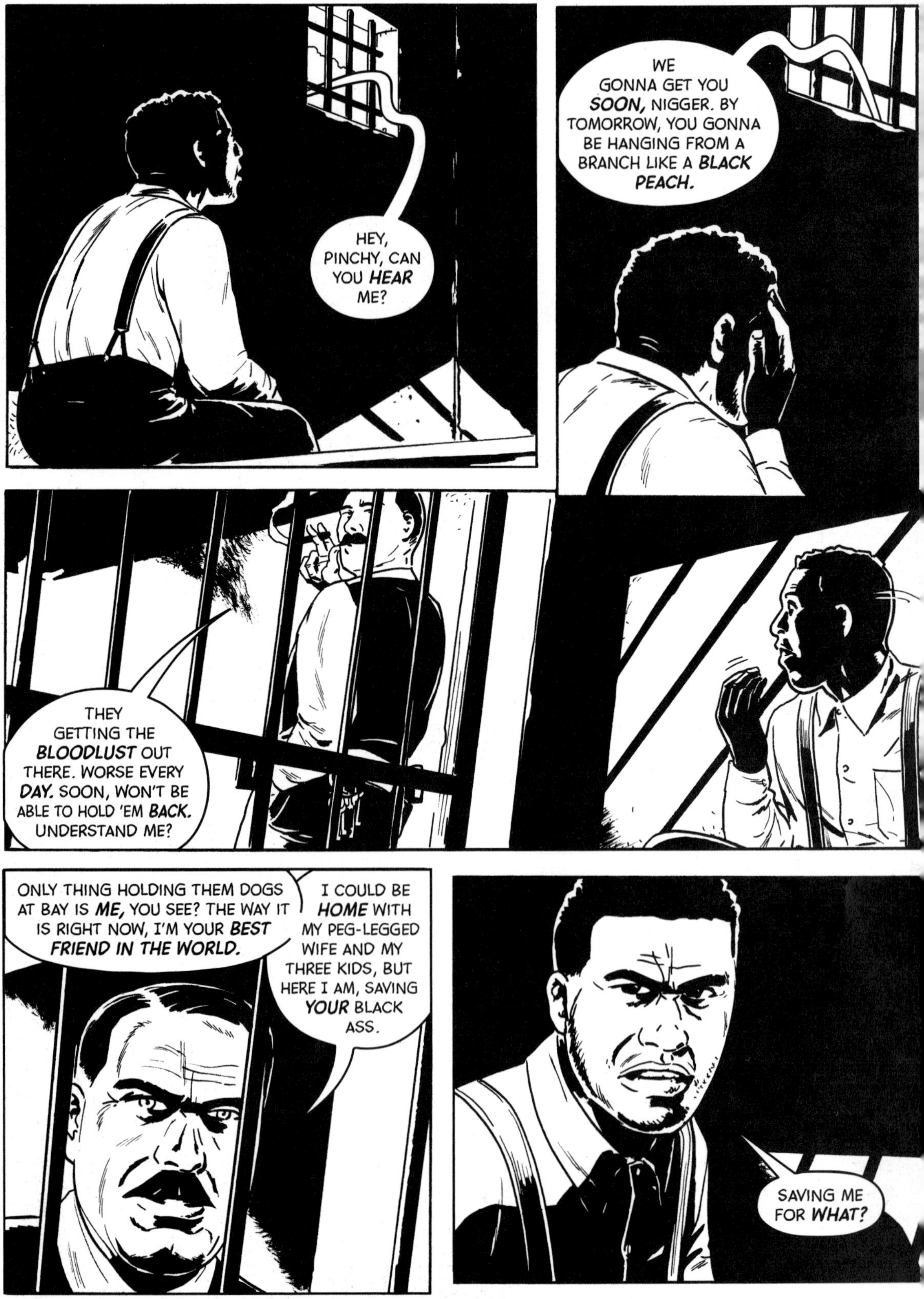
HEY, PINCHY, CAN YOU HEAR ME?
WE GONNA GET YOU SOON, NIGGER. BY TOMORROW, YOU GONNA BE HANGING FROM A BRANCH LIKE A BLACK PEACH.
THEY GETTING THE BLOODLUST OUT THERE. WORSE EVERY DAY. SOON, WON'T BE ABLE TO HOLD 'EM BACK. UNDERSTAND ME?
ONLY THING HOLDING THEM DOGS AT BAY IS ME, YOU SEE? THE WAY IT IS RIGHT NOW, I'M YOUR BEST FRIEND IN THE WORLD.
I COULD BE HOME WITH MY PEG-LEGGED WIFE AND MY THREE KIDS, BUT HERE I AM, SAVING YOUR BLACK ASS.
SAVING ME FOR WHAT?

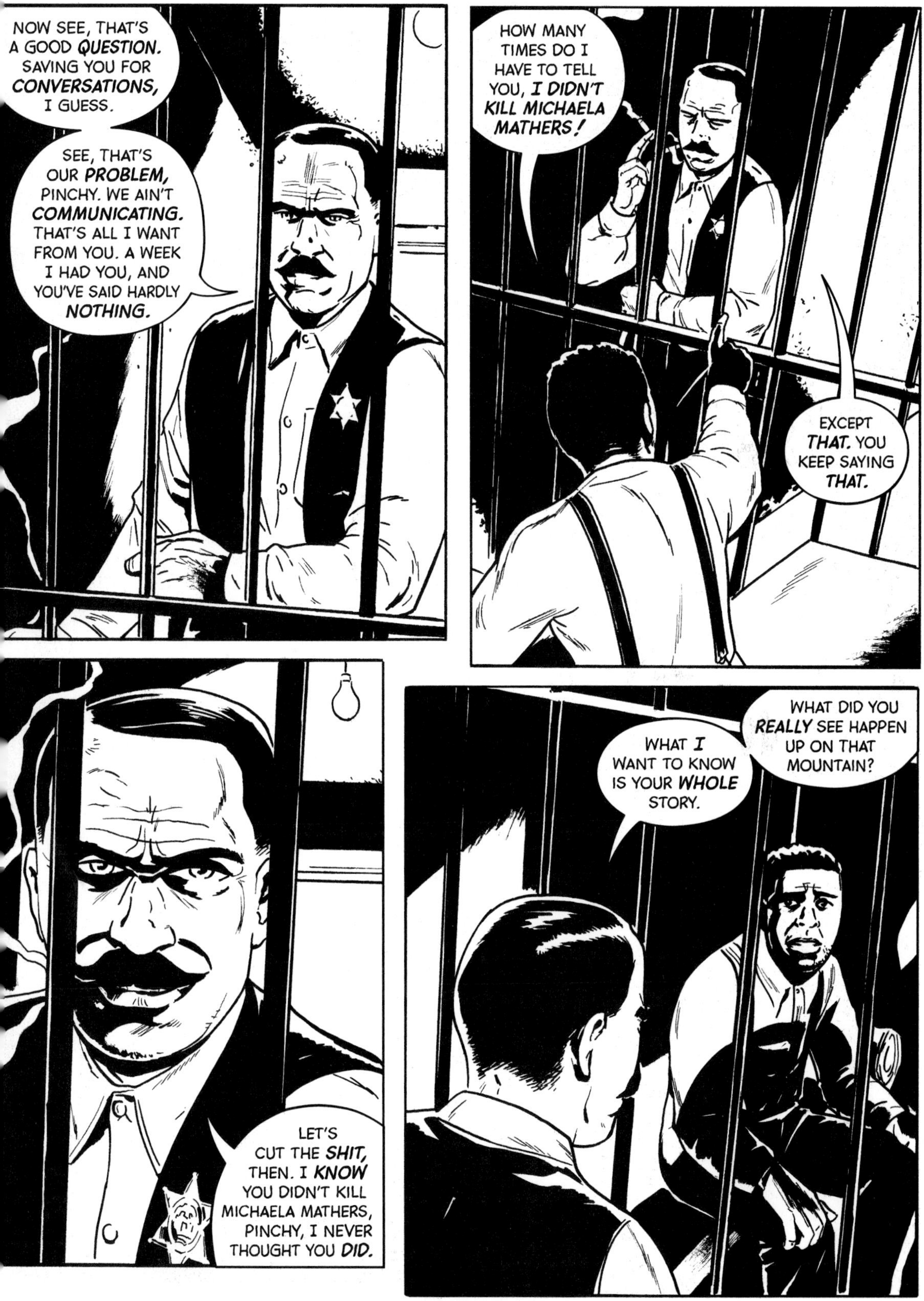
NOW SEE, THAT'S A GOOD QUESTION. SAVING YOU FOR CONVERSATIONS, I GUESS.
SEE, THAT'S OUR PROBLEM, PINCHY. WE AIN'T COMMUNICATING. THAT'S ALL I WANT FROM YOU. A WEEK I HAD YOU, AND YOU'VE SAID HARDLY NOTHING.
HOW MANY TIMES DO I HAVE TO TELL YOU, I DIDN'T KILL MICHAELA MATHERS!
EXCEPT THAT. YOU KEEP SAYING THAT.
LET'S CUT THE SHIT, THEN. I KNOW YOU DIDN'T KILL MICHAELA MATHERS, PINCHY, I NEVER THOUGHT YOU DID.
WHAT I WANT TO KNOW IS YOUR WHOLE STORY.
WHAT DID YOU REALLY SEE HAPPEN UP ON THAT MOUNTAIN?

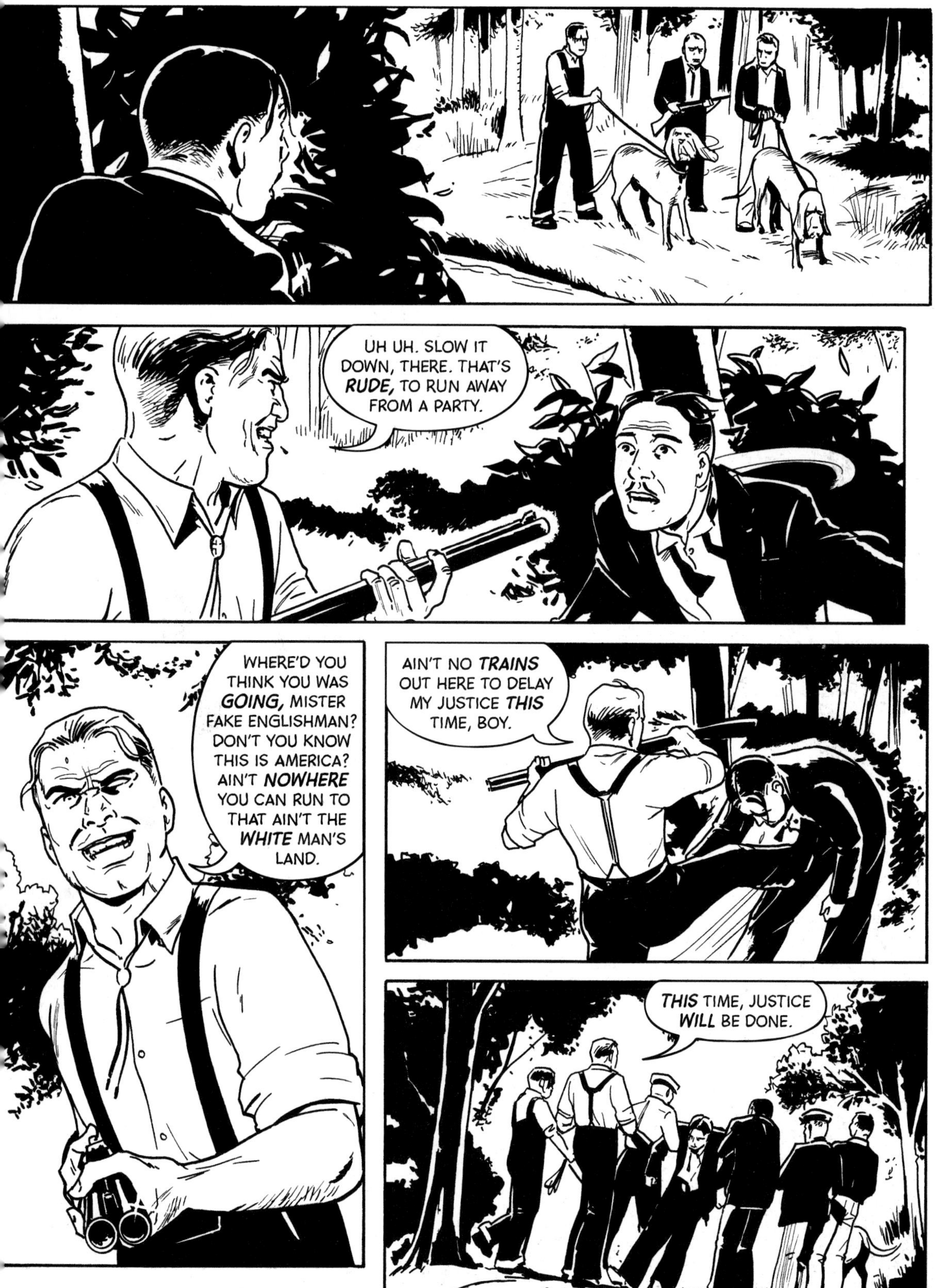
UH UH. SLOW IT DOWN, THERE. THAT'S RUDE, TO RUN AWAY FROM A PARTY.
WHERE'D YOU THINK YOU WAS GOING, MISTER FAKE ENGLISHMAN? DON'T YOU KNOW THIS IS AMERICA? AIN'T NOWHERE YOU CAN RUN TO THAT AIN'T THE WHITE MAN'S LAND.
AIN'T NO TRAINS OUT HERE TO DELAY MY JUSTICE THIS TIME, BOY.
THIS TIME, JUSTICE WILL BE DONE.

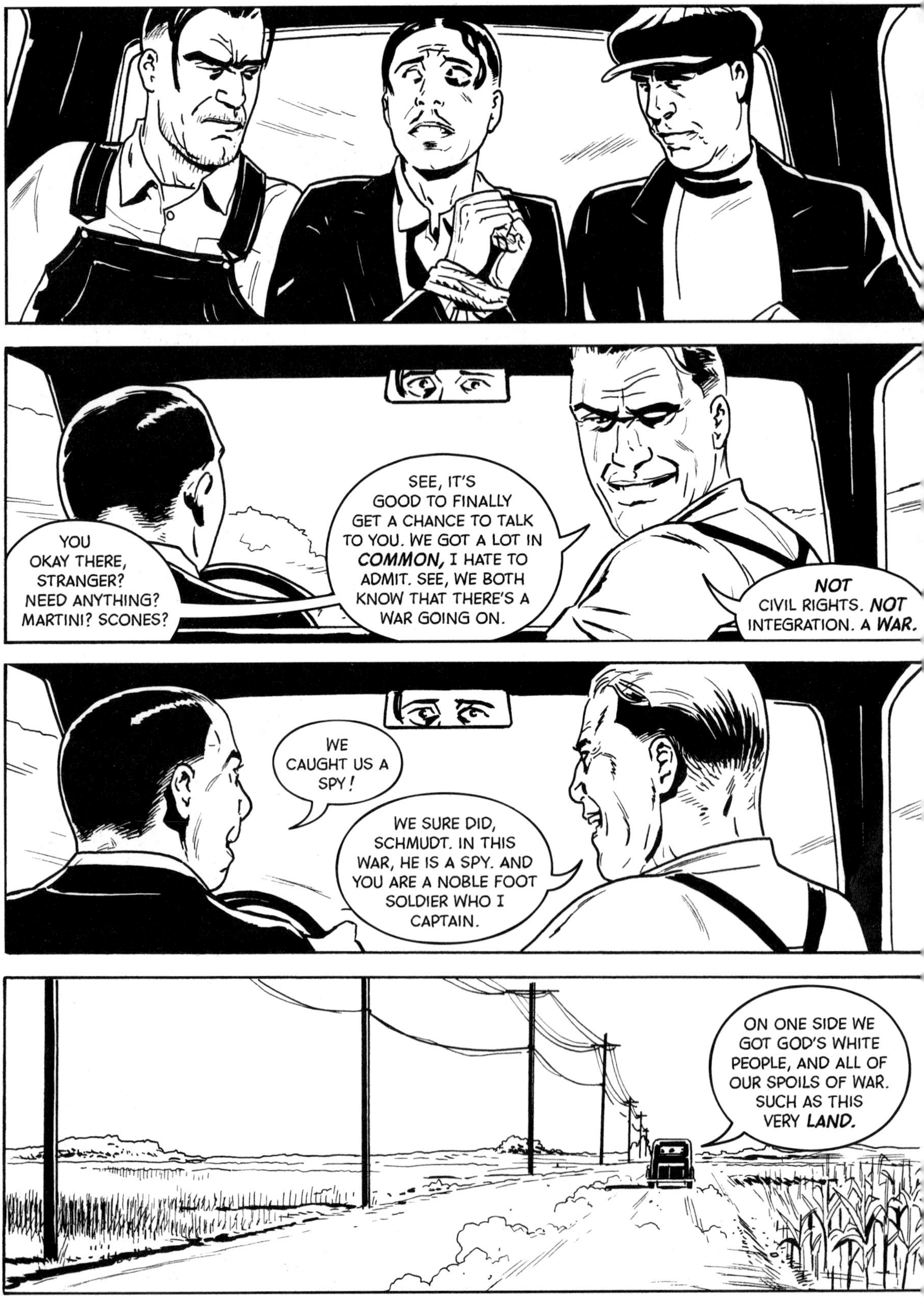

SEE, IT'S GOOD TO FINALLY GET A CHANCE TO TALK TO YOU. WE GOT A LOT IN **COMMON,** I HATE TO ADMIT. SEE, WE BOTH KNOW THAT THERE'S A WAR GOING ON.
YOU OKAY THERE, STRANGER? NEED ANYTHING? MARTINI? SCONES?
NOT CIVIL RIGHTS. **NOT** INTEGRATION. A **WAR.**
WE CAUGHT US A SPY!
WE SURE DID, SCHMUDT. IN THIS WAR, HE IS A SPY. AND YOU ARE A NOBLE FOOT SOLDIER WHO I CAPTAIN.
ON ONE SIDE WE GOT GOD'S WHITE PEOPLE, AND ALL OF OUR SPOILS OF WAR. SUCH AS THIS VERY **LAND.**

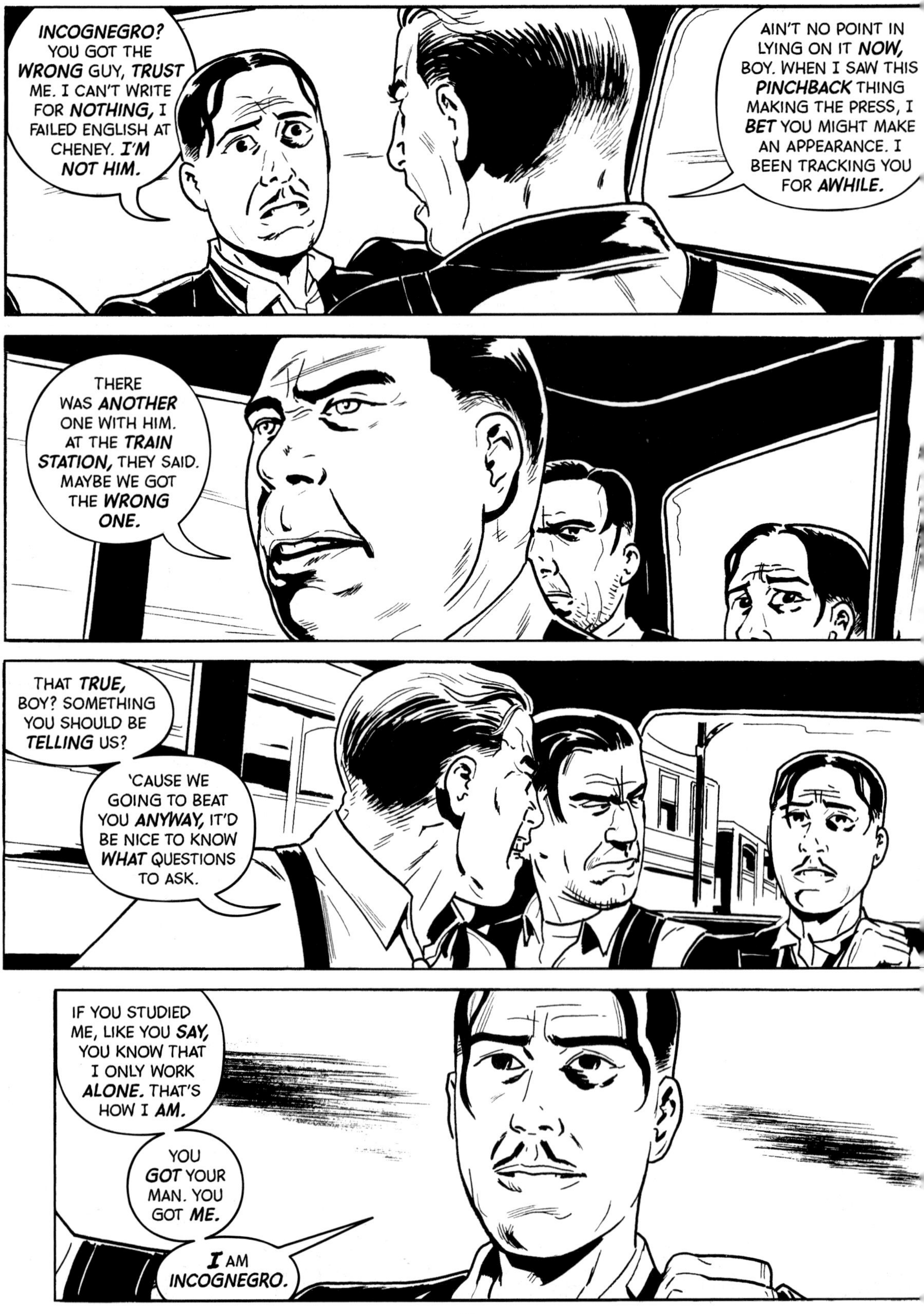
INCOGNEGRO? YOU GOT THE WRONG GUY, TRUST ME. I CAN'T WRITE FOR NOTHING, I FAILED ENGLISH AT CHENEY. I'M NOT HIM.
AIN'T NO POINT IN LYING ON IT NOW, BOY. WHEN I SAW THIS PINCHBACK THING MAKING THE PRESS, I BET YOU MIGHT MAKE AN APPEARANCE. I BEEN TRACKING YOU FOR AWHILE.
THERE WAS ANOTHER ONE WITH HIM. AT THE TRAIN STATION, THEY SAID. MAYBE WE GOT THE WRONG ONE.
THAT TRUE, BOY? SOMETHING YOU SHOULD BE TELLING US?
'CAUSE WE GOING TO BEAT YOU ANYWAY, IT'D BE NICE TO KNOW WHAT QUESTIONS TO ASK.
IF YOU STUDIED ME, LIKE YOU SAY, YOU KNOW THAT I ONLY WORK ALONE. THAT'S HOW I AM.
YOU GOT YOUR MAN. YOU GOT ME.
I AM INCOGNEGRO.

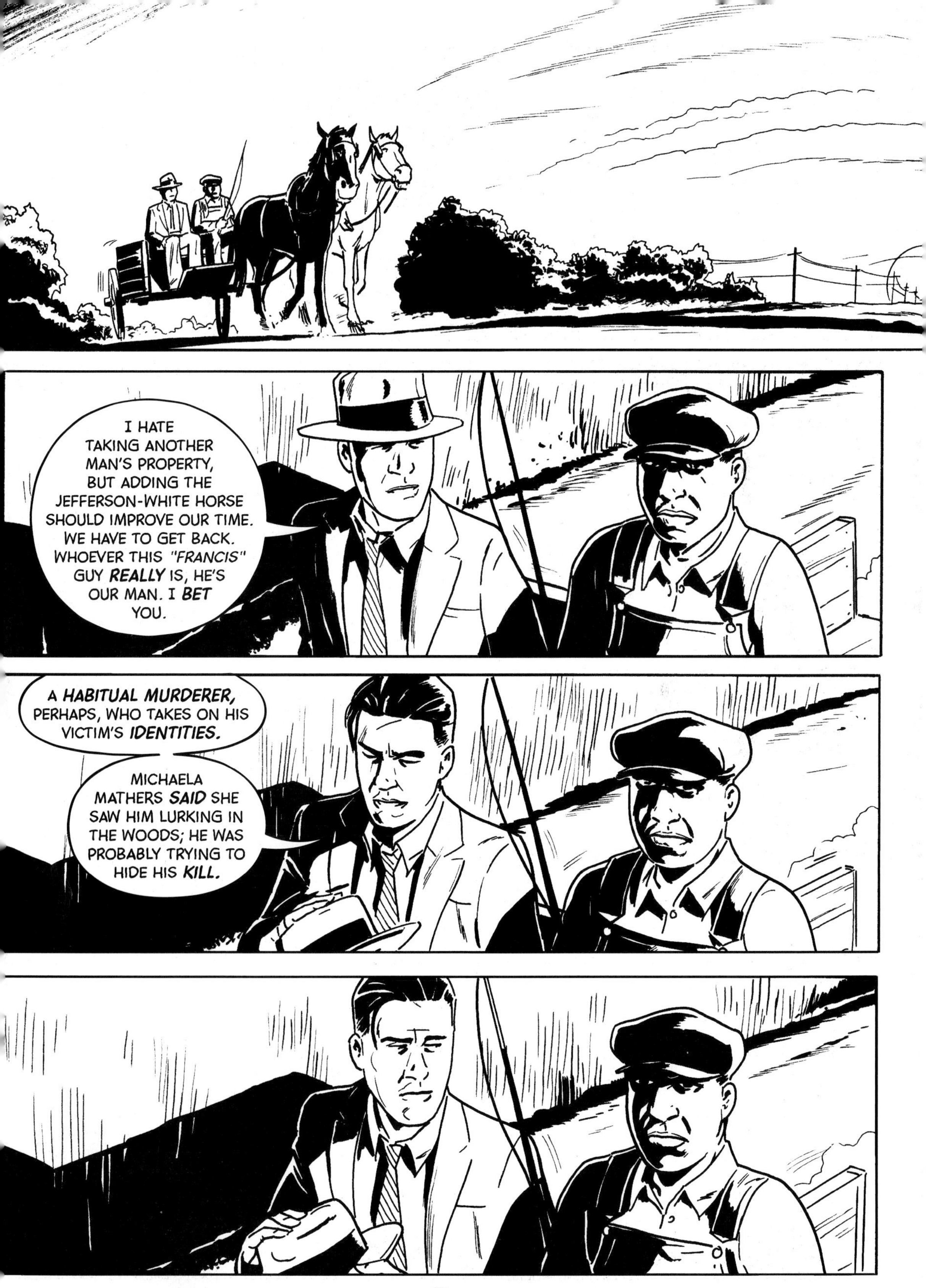
I HATE TAKING ANOTHER MAN'S PROPERTY, BUT ADDING THE JEFFERSON-WHITE HORSE SHOULD IMPROVE OUR TIME. WE HAVE TO GET BACK. WHOEVER THIS "FRANCIS" GUY REALLY IS, HE'S OUR MAN. I BET YOU.
A HABITUAL MURDERER, PERHAPS, WHO TAKES ON HIS VICTIM'S IDENTITIES.
MICHAELA MATHERS SAID SHE SAW HIM LURKING IN THE WOODS; HE WAS PROBABLY TRYING TO HIDE HIS KILL.

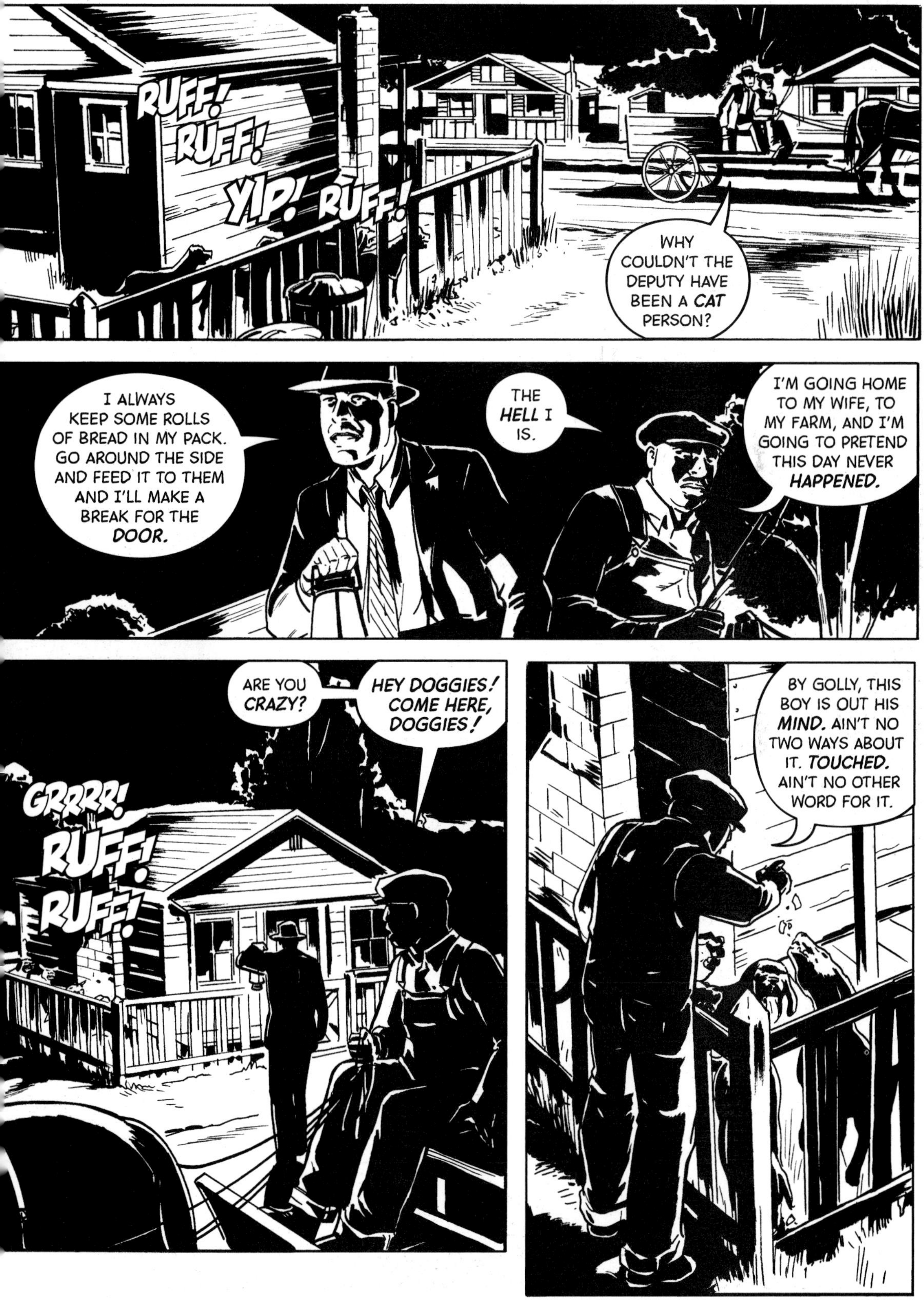
RUFF! RUFF!
YIP! RUFF!
WHY COULDN'T THE DEPUTY HAVE BEEN A CAT PERSON?
I ALWAYS KEEP SOME ROLLS OF BREAD IN MY PACK. GO AROUND THE SIDE AND FEED IT TO THEM AND I'LL MAKE A BREAK FOR THE DOOR.
THE HELL I IS.
I'M GOING HOME TO MY WIFE, TO MY FARM, AND I'M GOING TO PRETEND THIS DAY NEVER HAPPENED.
GRRRR! RUFF! RUFF!
HEY DOGGIES! COME HERE, DOGGIES!
ARE YOU CRAZY?
BY GOLLY, THIS BOY IS OUT HIS MIND. AIN'T NO TWO WAYS ABOUT IT. TOUCHED. AIN'T NO OTHER WORD FOR IT.

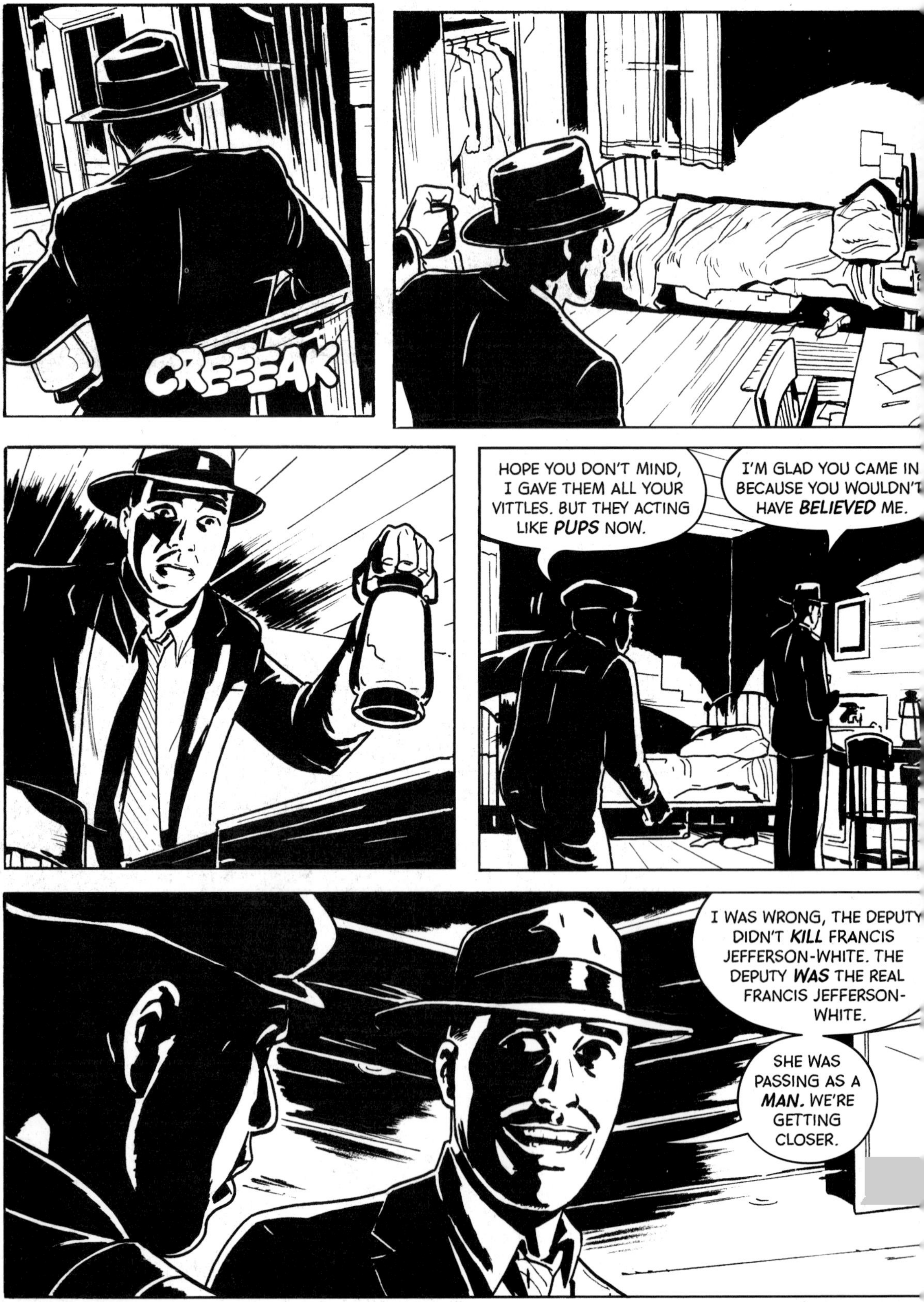
CREEEAK
HOPE YOU DON'T MIND, I GAVE THEM ALL YOUR VITTLES. BUT THEY ACTING LIKE PUPS NOW.
I'M GLAD YOU CAME IN BECAUSE YOU WOULDN'T HAVE BELIEVED ME.
I WAS WRONG, THE DEPUTY DIDN'T KILL FRANCIS JEFFERSON-WHITE. THE DEPUTY WAS THE REAL FRANCIS JEFFERSON-WHITE.
SHE WAS PASSING AS A MAN. WE'RE GETTING CLOSER.

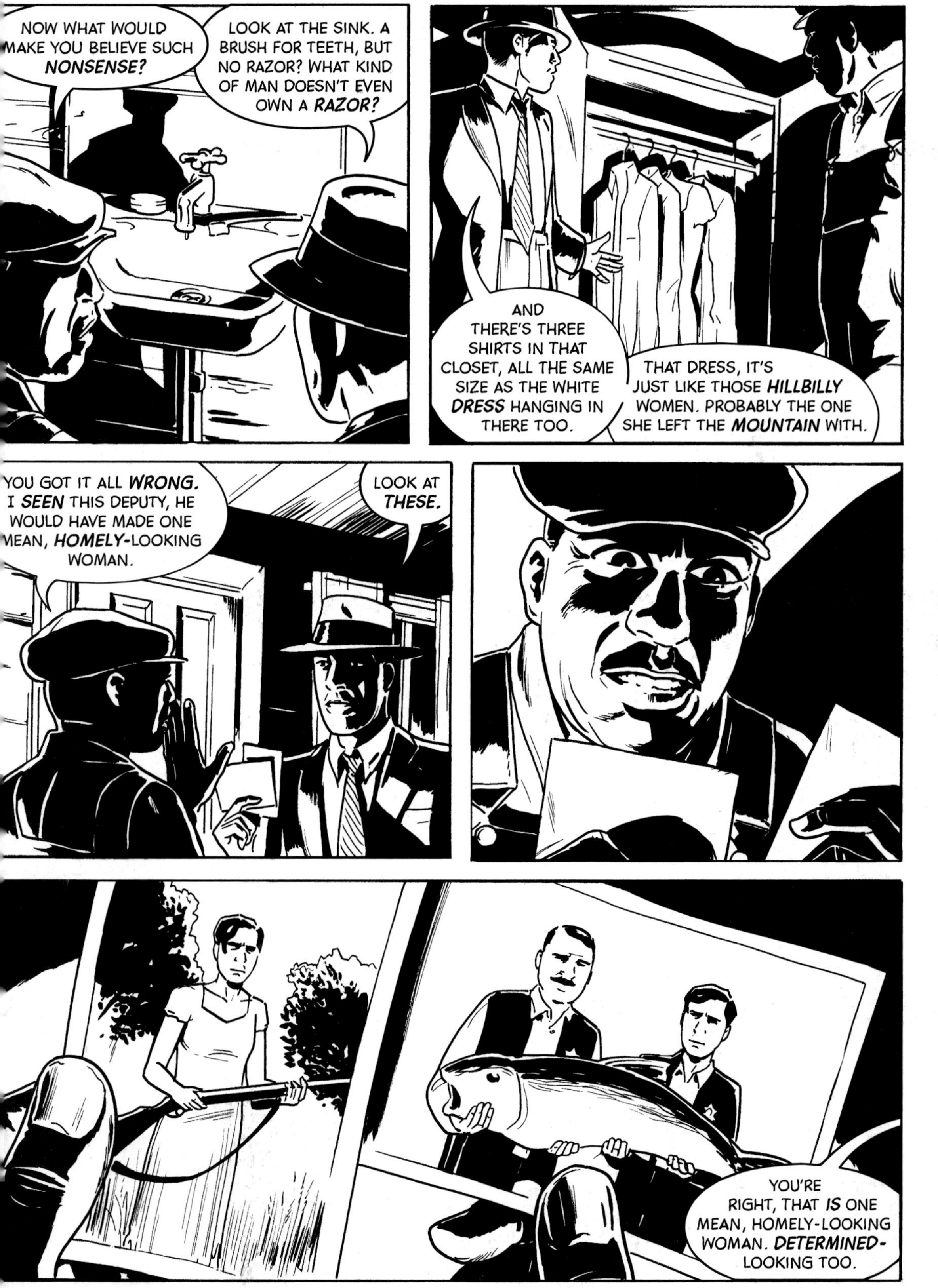
NOW WHAT WOULD MAKE YOU BELIEVE SUCH NONSENSE?
LOOK AT THE SINK. A BRUSH FOR TEETH, BUT NO RAZOR? WHAT KIND OF MAN DOESN'T EVEN OWN A RAZOR?
AND THERE'S THREE SHIRTS IN THAT CLOSET, ALL THE SAME SIZE AS THE WHITE DRESS HANGING IN THERE TOO.
THAT DRESS, IT'S JUST LIKE THOSE HILLBILLY WOMEN. PROBABLY THE ONE SHE LEFT THE MOUNTAIN WITH.
YOU GOT IT ALL WRONG. I SEEN THIS DEPUTY, HE WOULD HAVE MADE ONE MEAN, HOMELY-LOOKING WOMAN.
LOOK AT THESE.
YOU'RE RIGHT, THAT IS ONE MEAN, HOMELY-LOOKING WOMAN. DETERMINED-LOOKING TOO.

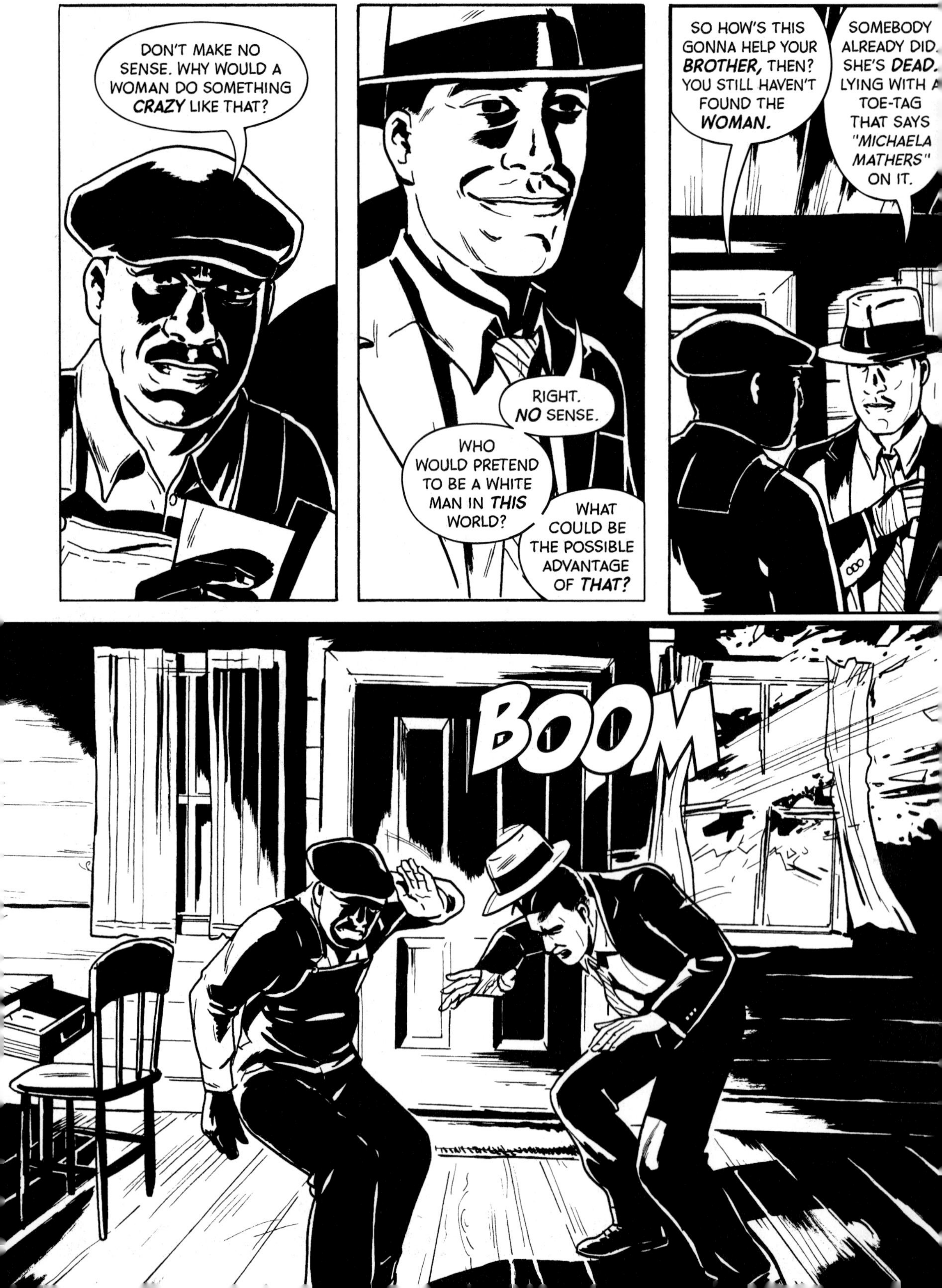
DON'T MAKE NO SENSE. WHY WOULD A WOMAN DO SOMETHING CRAZY LIKE THAT?
RIGHT. NO SENSE.
WHO WOULD PRETEND TO BE A WHITE MAN IN THIS WORLD?
WHAT COULD BE THE POSSIBLE ADVANTAGE OF THAT?
SO HOW'S THIS GONNA HELP YOUR BROTHER, THEN? YOU STILL HAVEN'T FOUND THE WOMAN.
SOMEBODY ALREADY DID. SHE'S DEAD. LYING WITH A TOE-TAG THAT SAYS "MICHAELA MATHERS" ON IT.
BOOM

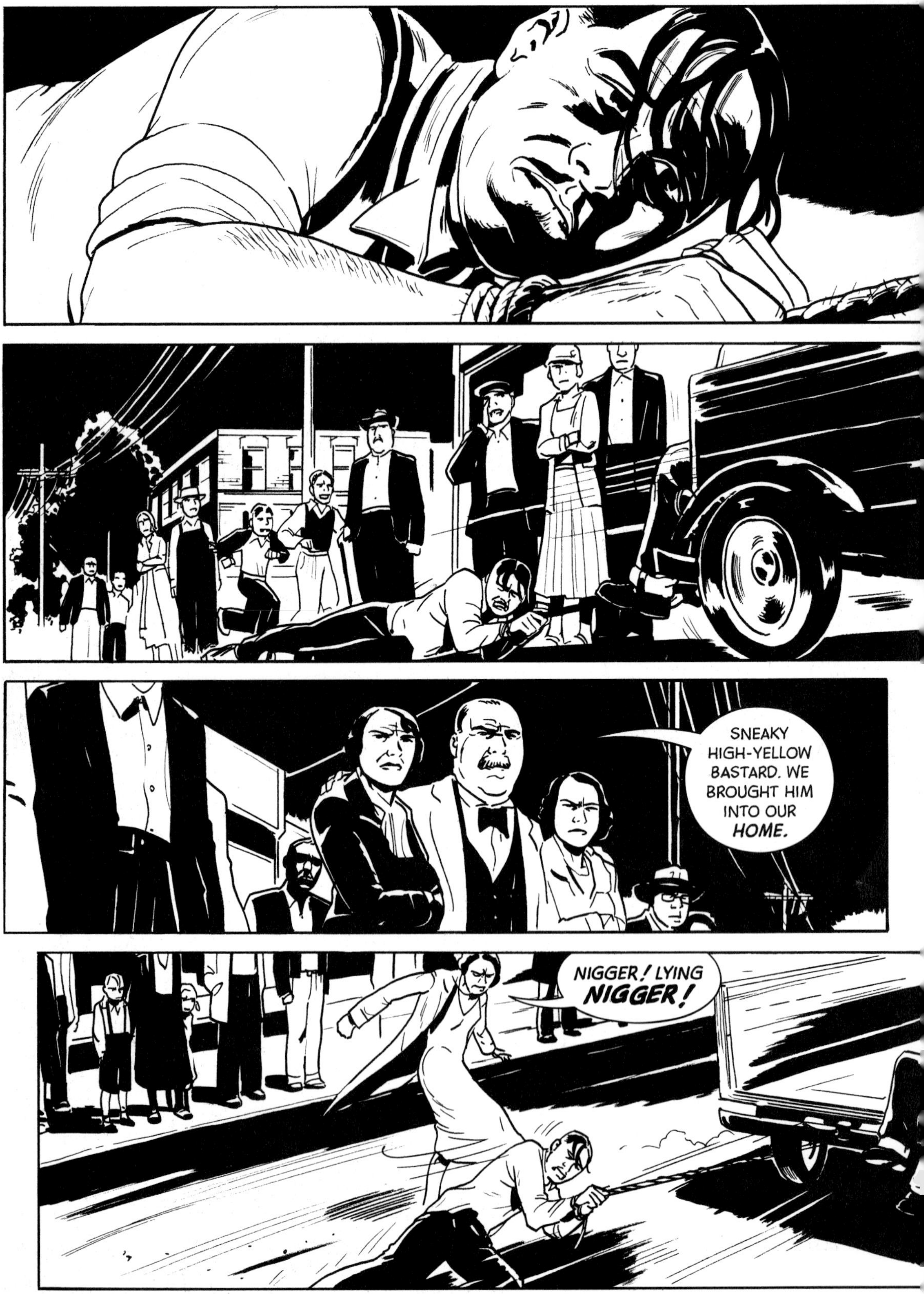
SNEAKY HIGH-YELLOW BASTARD. WE BROUGHT HIM INTO OUR HOME.
NIGGER! LYING NIGGER!

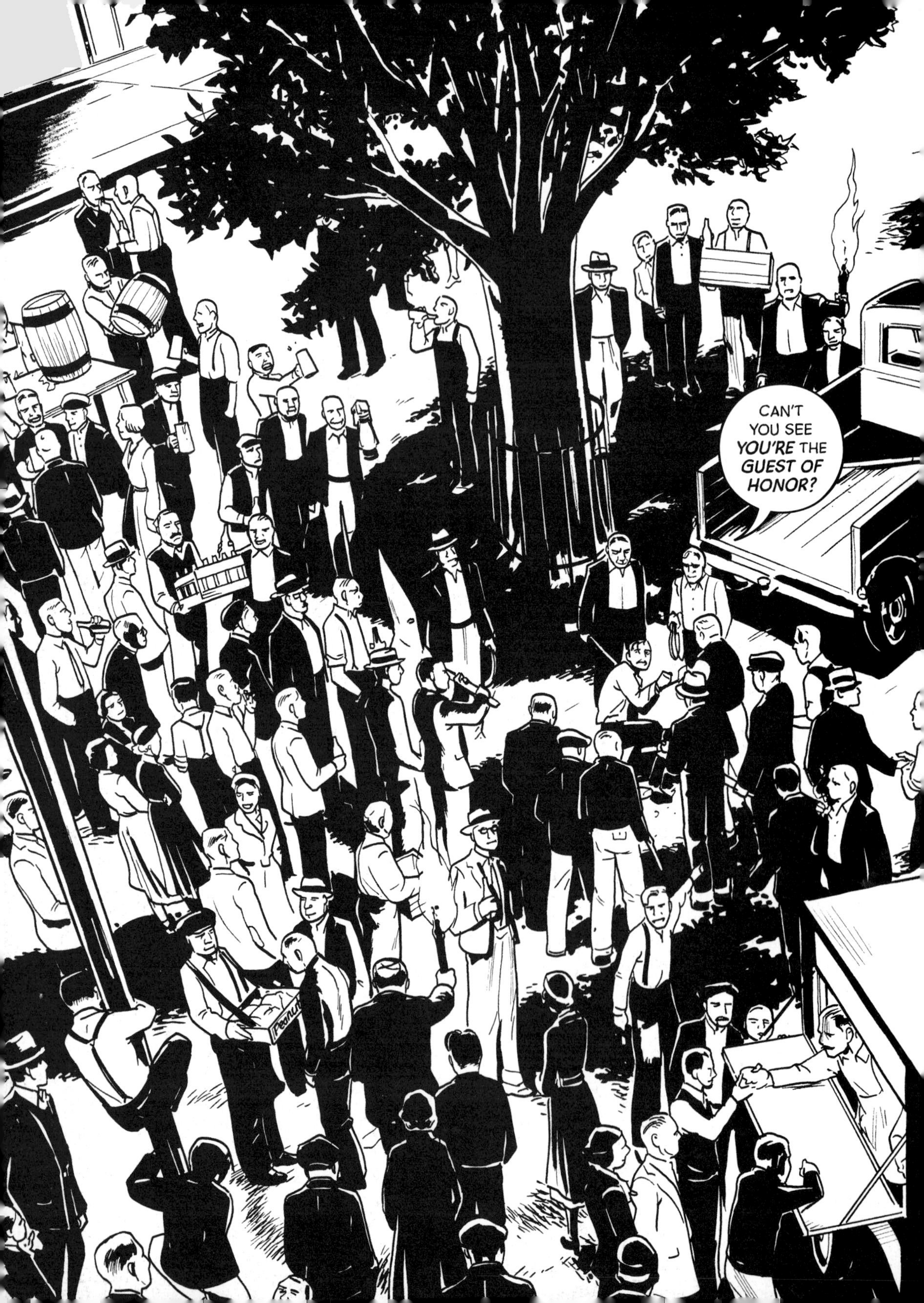
CAN'T YOU SEE *YOU'RE* THE *GUEST OF HONOR?*

PART III

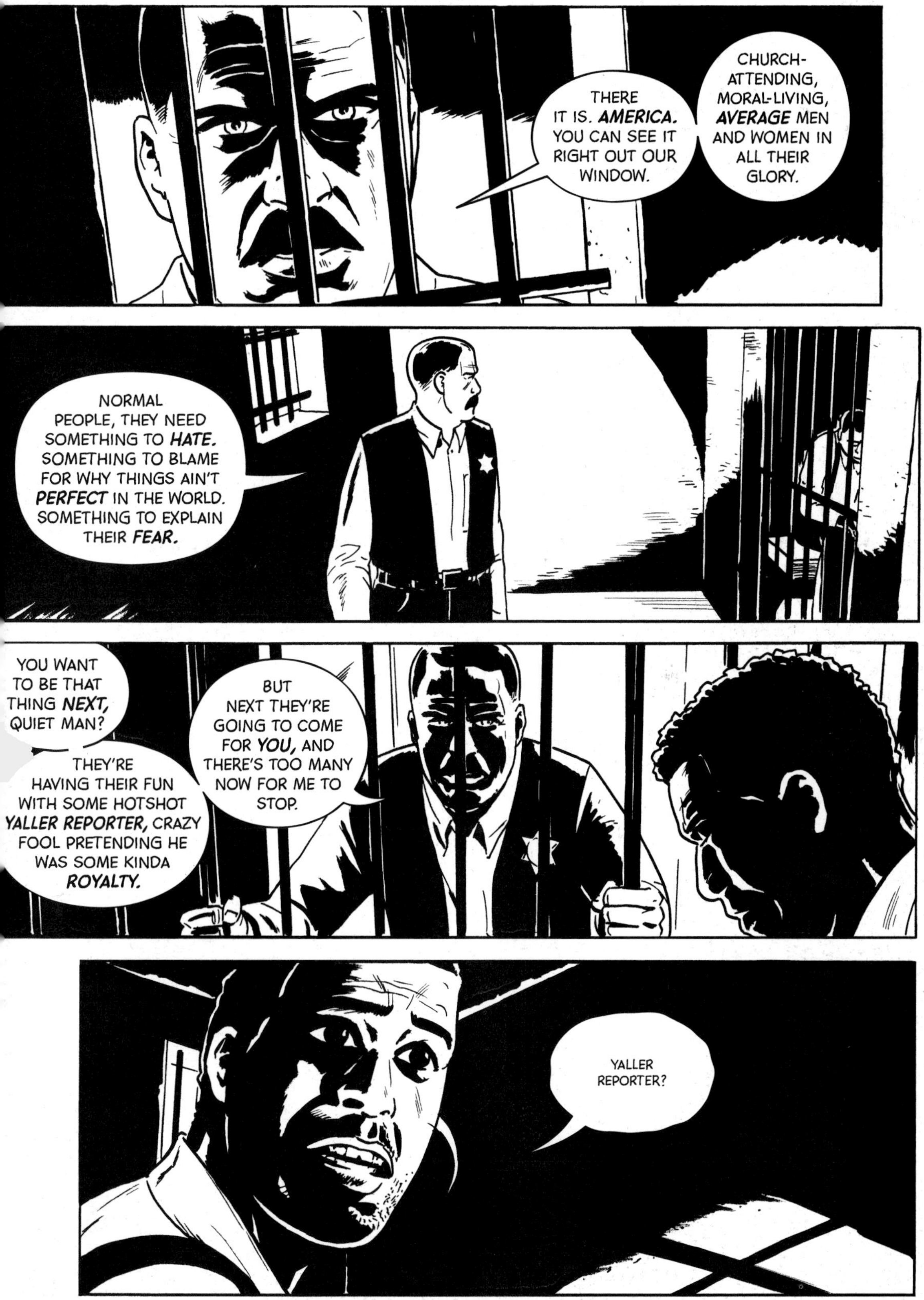
THERE IT IS. AMERICA. YOU CAN SEE IT RIGHT OUT OUR WINDOW.
CHURCH-ATTENDING, MORAL-LIVING, AVERAGE MEN AND WOMEN IN ALL THEIR GLORY.
NORMAL PEOPLE, THEY NEED SOMETHING TO HATE. SOMETHING TO BLAME FOR WHY THINGS AIN'T PERFECT IN THE WORLD. SOMETHING TO EXPLAIN THEIR FEAR.
YOU WANT TO BE THAT THING NEXT, QUIET MAN?
THEY'RE HAVING THEIR FUN WITH SOME HOTSHOT YALLER REPORTER, CRAZY FOOL PRETENDING HE WAS SOME KINDA ROYALTY.
BUT NEXT THEY'RE GOING TO COME FOR YOU, AND THERE'S TOO MANY NOW FOR ME TO STOP.
YALLER REPORTER?

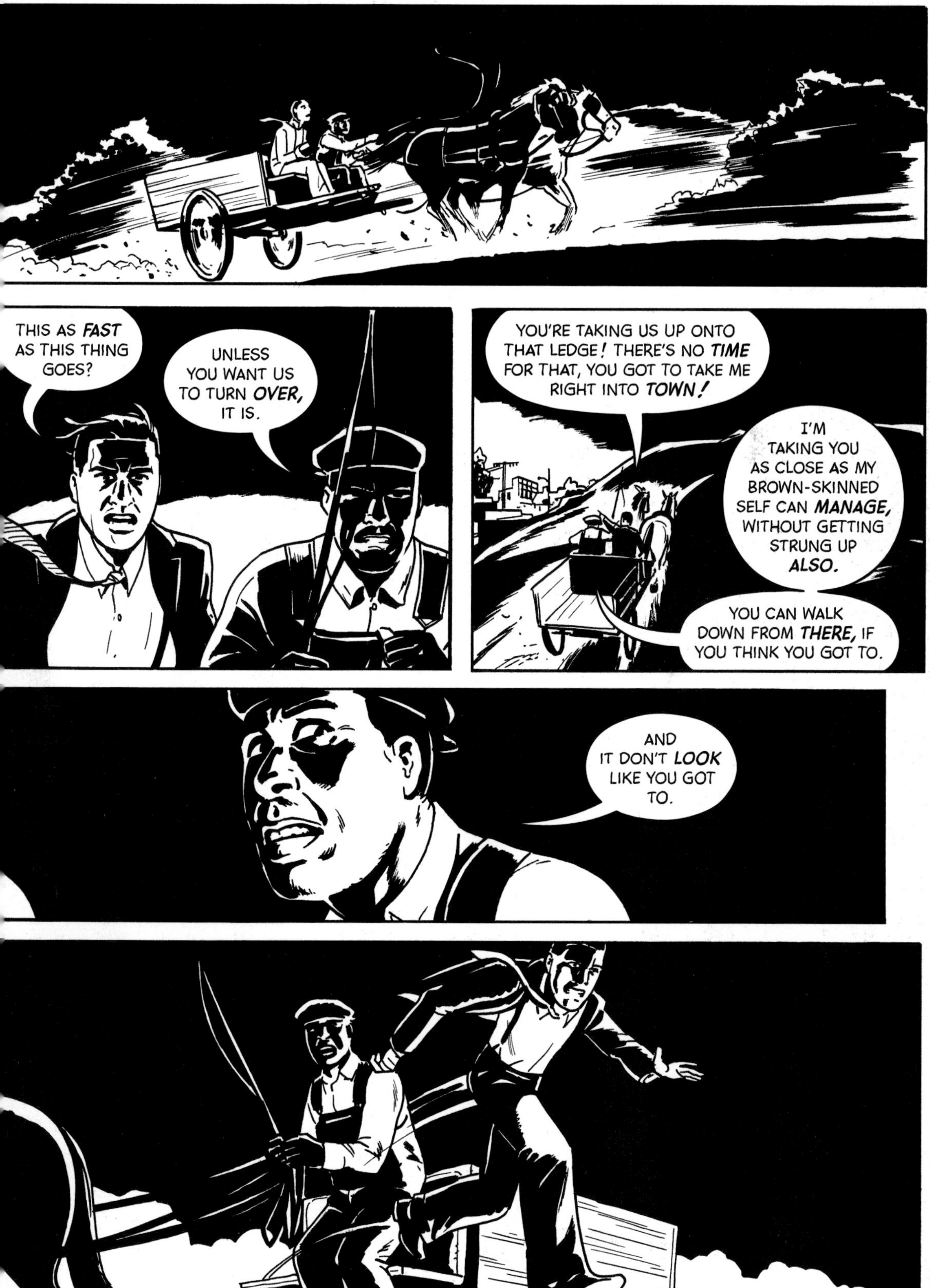
THIS AS FAST AS THIS THING GOES?
UNLESS YOU WANT US TO TURN OVER, IT IS.
YOU'RE TAKING US UP ONTO THAT LEDGE! THERE'S NO TIME FOR THAT, YOU GOT TO TAKE ME RIGHT INTO TOWN!
I'M TAKING YOU AS CLOSE AS MY BROWN-SKINNED SELF CAN MANAGE, WITHOUT GETTING STRUNG UP ALSO.
YOU CAN WALK DOWN FROM THERE, IF YOU THINK YOU GOT TO.
AND IT DON'T LOOK LIKE YOU GOT TO.

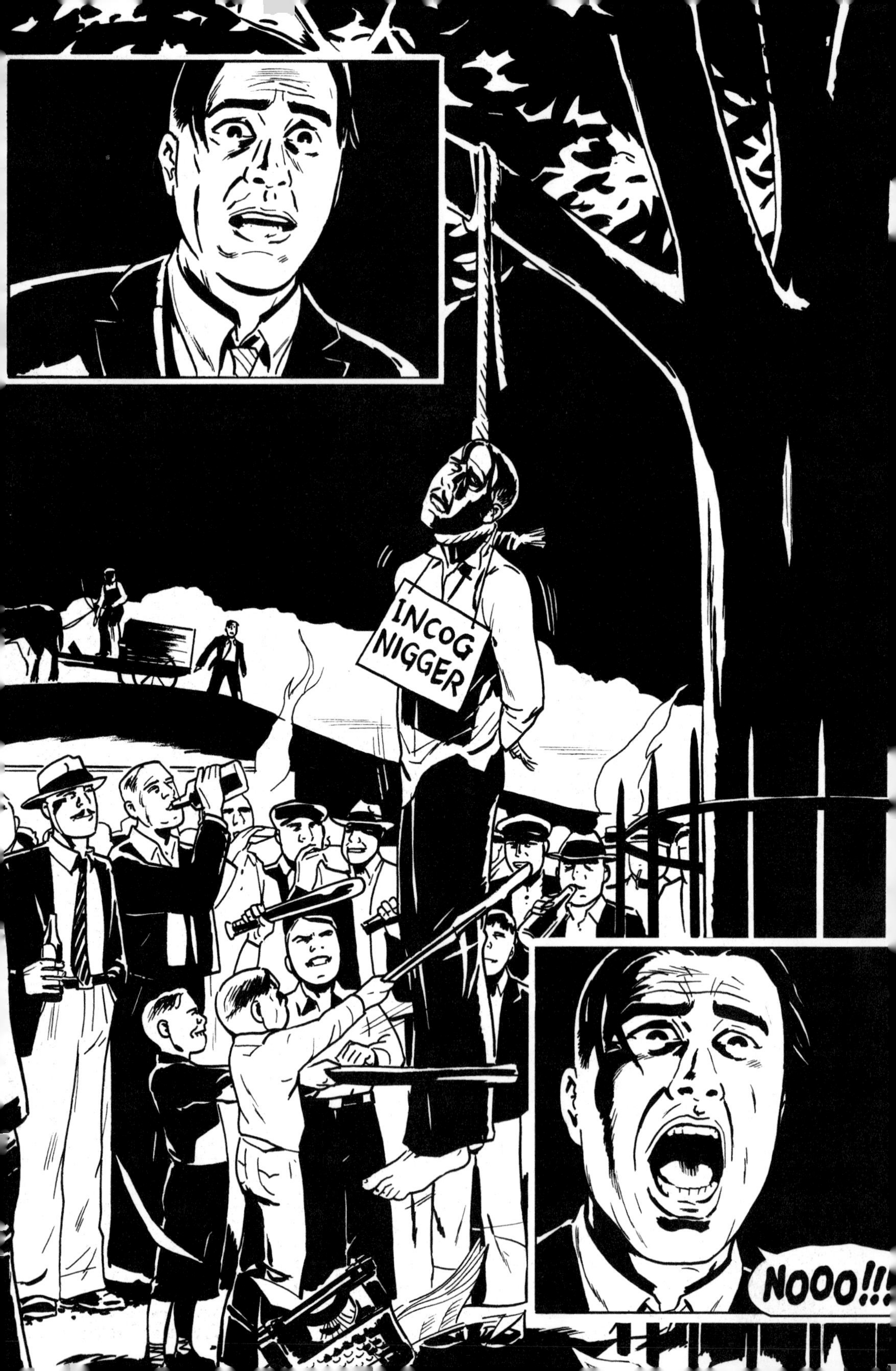
INCOG
NIGGER
NOOO!!

MMPH!

CONTROL YOURSELF, MAN. YOU ABOUT TO *JOIN* HIM UP IN THAT TREE, SO JUST CALM YOURSELF *DOWN.*

THAT'S *CARL.* THAT'S MY *FRIEND.* THAT'S MY *BEST FRIEND.* THEY *KILLED* HIM.

WHAT'S AN "INCOGNIGGER"?

THEY THOUGHT IT WAS ME. THEY THOUGHT *HE* WAS *ME.* THEY THOUGHT THEY HAD *INCOGNEGRO.*

I KILLED HIM. *I* GOT HIM KILLED. MY ACTIONS, MY WORK. *THAT'S* WHAT KILLED HIM.

PULL YOURSELF TOGETHER. *LOOK* AT THAT SCENE. *LOOK* AT WHAT THOSE CRACKERS DID. *LOOK* AT THEM LAUGHING.

YOU KILLED HIM? COULD YOU EVEN BE *CAPABLE* OF ACTING LIKE THAT?

LET'S GET *OUT* OF HERE. YOU CAN TAKE THE NEXT TRAIN. *ENOUGH* BLOOD DONE POURED. IT'S *OVER.*

NO.

NO. EVERYBODY IN TOWN IS OUT HERE. THAT MEANS THE *JAIL* ISN'T BEING *WATCHED.* THIS IS MY *CHANCE.*

I CAME FOR MY BROTHER. I'M *GETTING* MY BROTHER. *THEN* I'M GOING HOME.

SUIT YOURSELF THEN. I *DONE* MY BIT. YOU WANT TO KEEP ACTING A FOOL, YOU ON YOUR *OWN.*

WOULDN'T ASK OTHERWISE. I CAN FIGURE IT OUT. BUT JUST ONE MORE QUESTION.

HOW MUCH YOU WANT FOR ONE OF THEM BROKEN-DOWN *HORSES?*

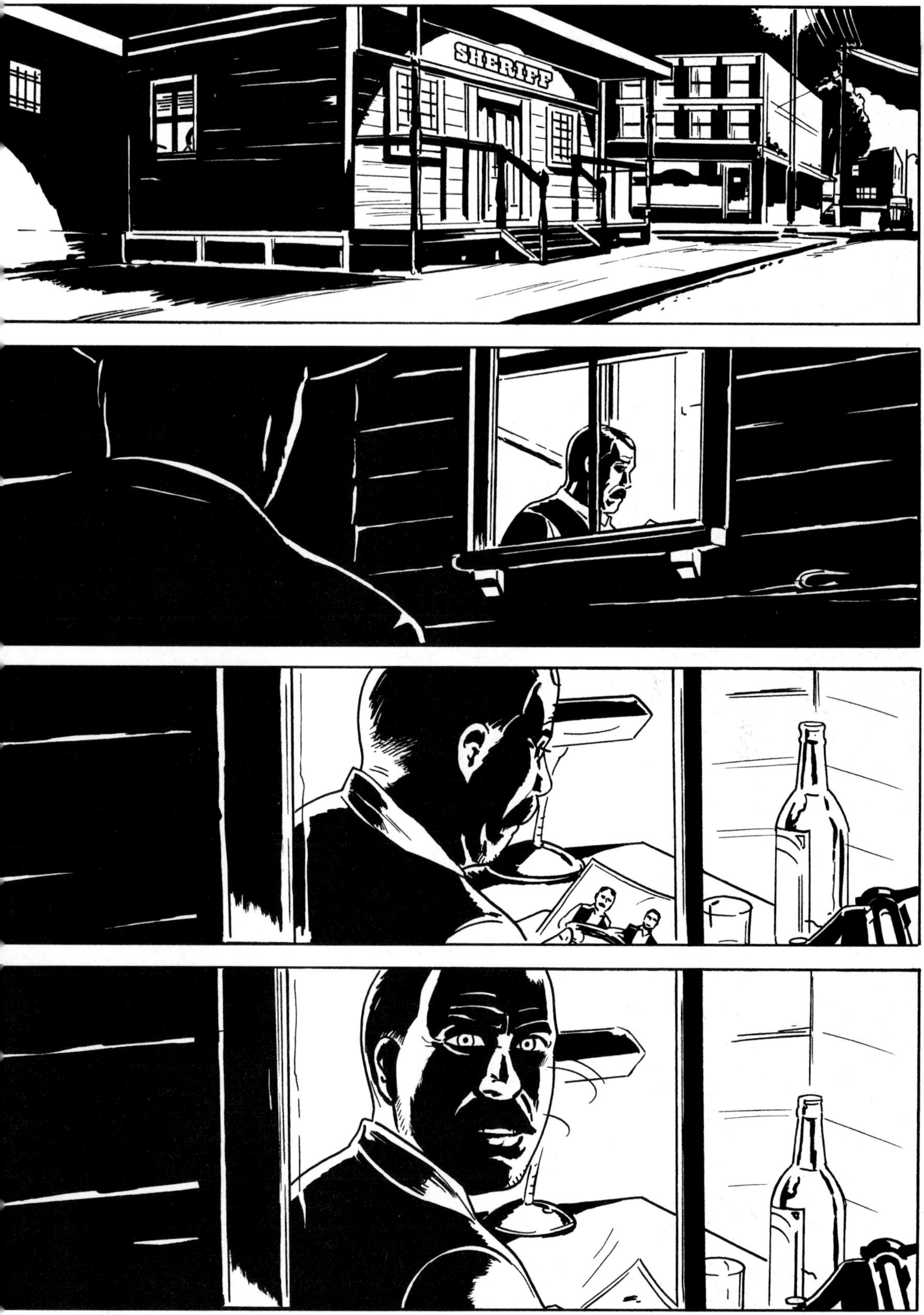
SHERIFF

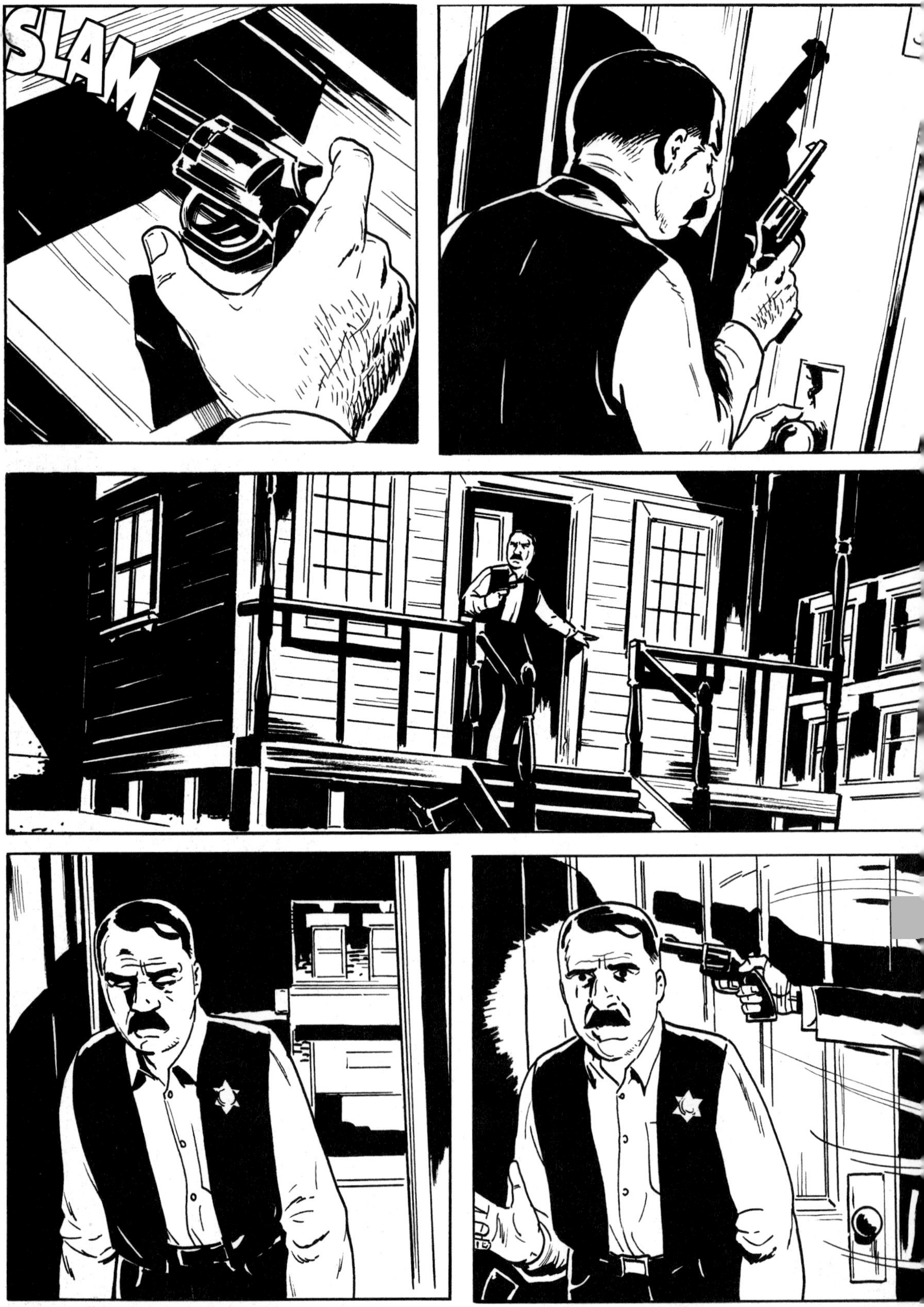
SLAM

I GUESS AFTER ALL THIS IS DONE, THEY'RE GOING TO SAY I SHOULD HAVE LET THEM LYNCH HIM WHEN I HAD THE *CHANCE*.

BUT YOU KNOW YOU *SHOULDN'T*. BECAUSE YOU KNOW PINCHY'S *NOT* A MURDERER.

OH I *DO*, DO I? IS *THAT* WHAT YOU THINK?

WHAT *I* THINK IS THAT YOU AND DEPUTY FRANCIS JEFFERSON-WHITE WERE A LOT *CLOSER* THAN ANYBODY ELSE WOULD *EVER* GUESS.

ZANE? IS THAT YOU?

YOU'RE *ALIVE!* I *KNEW* IT! I *KNEW* YOU WERE TOO SMART FOR THESE CRACKERS.

YOU DON'T KNOW A GODDAMN *THING*.

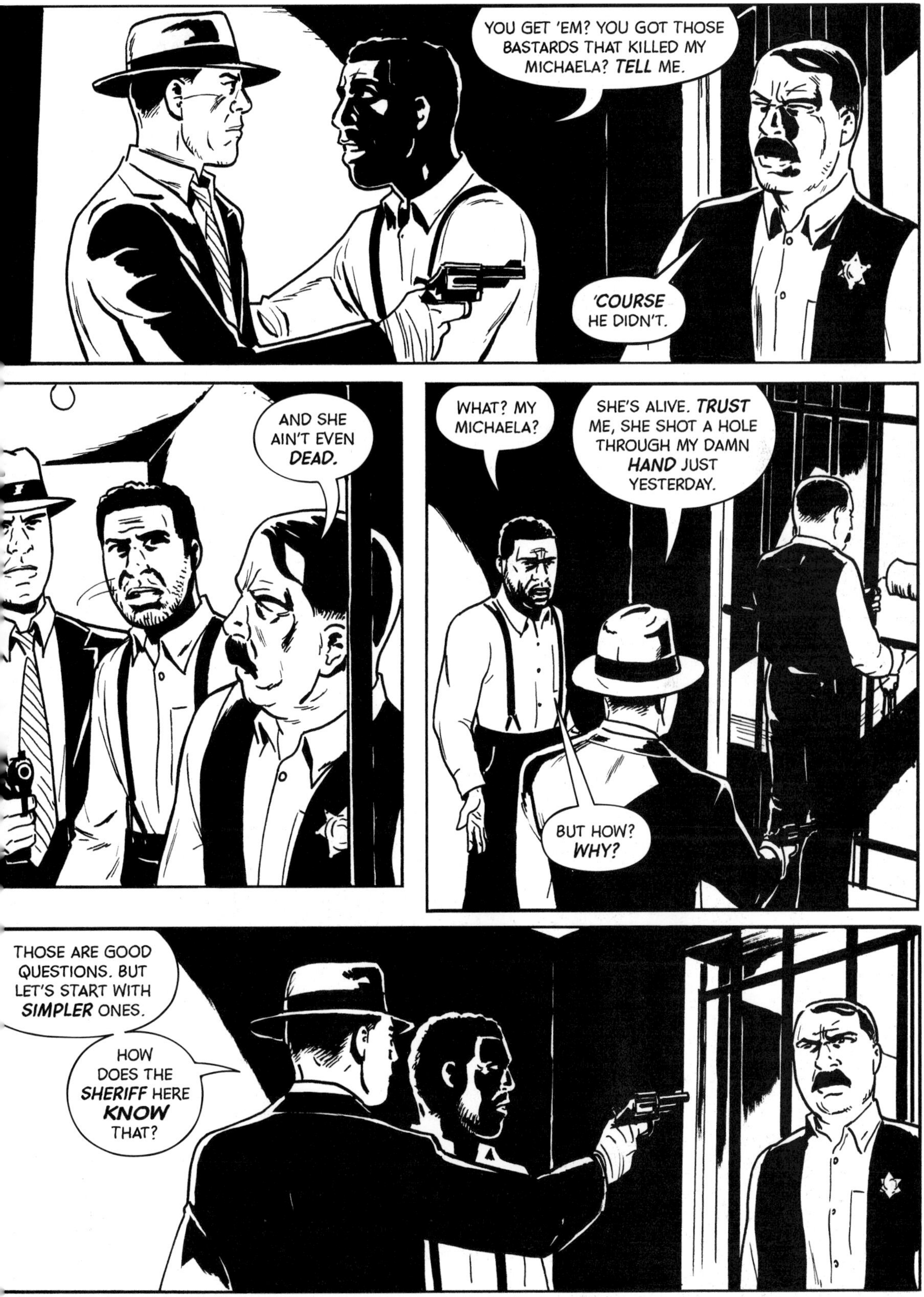
YOU GET 'EM? YOU GOT THOSE BASTARDS THAT KILLED MY MICHAELA? TELL ME.
'COURSE HE DIDN'T.
AND SHE AIN'T EVEN DEAD.
WHAT? MY MICHAELA?
SHE'S ALIVE. TRUST ME, SHE SHOT A HOLE THROUGH MY DAMN HAND JUST YESTERDAY.
BUT HOW? WHY?
THOSE ARE GOOD QUESTIONS. BUT LET'S START WITH SIMPLER ONES.
HOW DOES THE SHERIFF HERE KNOW THAT?

YOU TWO, YOU'RE JUST LIKE EVERYBODY *ELSE* IN THIS BLOOD-SOAKED TOWN. YOU'RE HYPOCRITES.

HYPOCRITES?! YOU ARRESTED MY BROTHER FOR A CRIME YOU *KNOW* HE HAD NOTHING TO DO WITH, DRAGGING ME FROM THE SANITY OF NEW YORK TO GET SHOT AT IN THIS SHIT HOLE. *YOUR* ACTIONS RESULTED IN THE DEATH OF MY *BEST FRIEND.*

IF YOU WANT ME TO *SHOOT* YOU, JUST *ASK.* BUT DON'T *INSULT* ME.

THAT'S RICH. SO *TELL* ME, HOW DO *I* KNOW YOUR SCUMBAG BROTHER HAD NOTHING TO DO WITH THE MURDER?

BECAUSE *YOU'RE* THE ONE THAT KILLED HER.

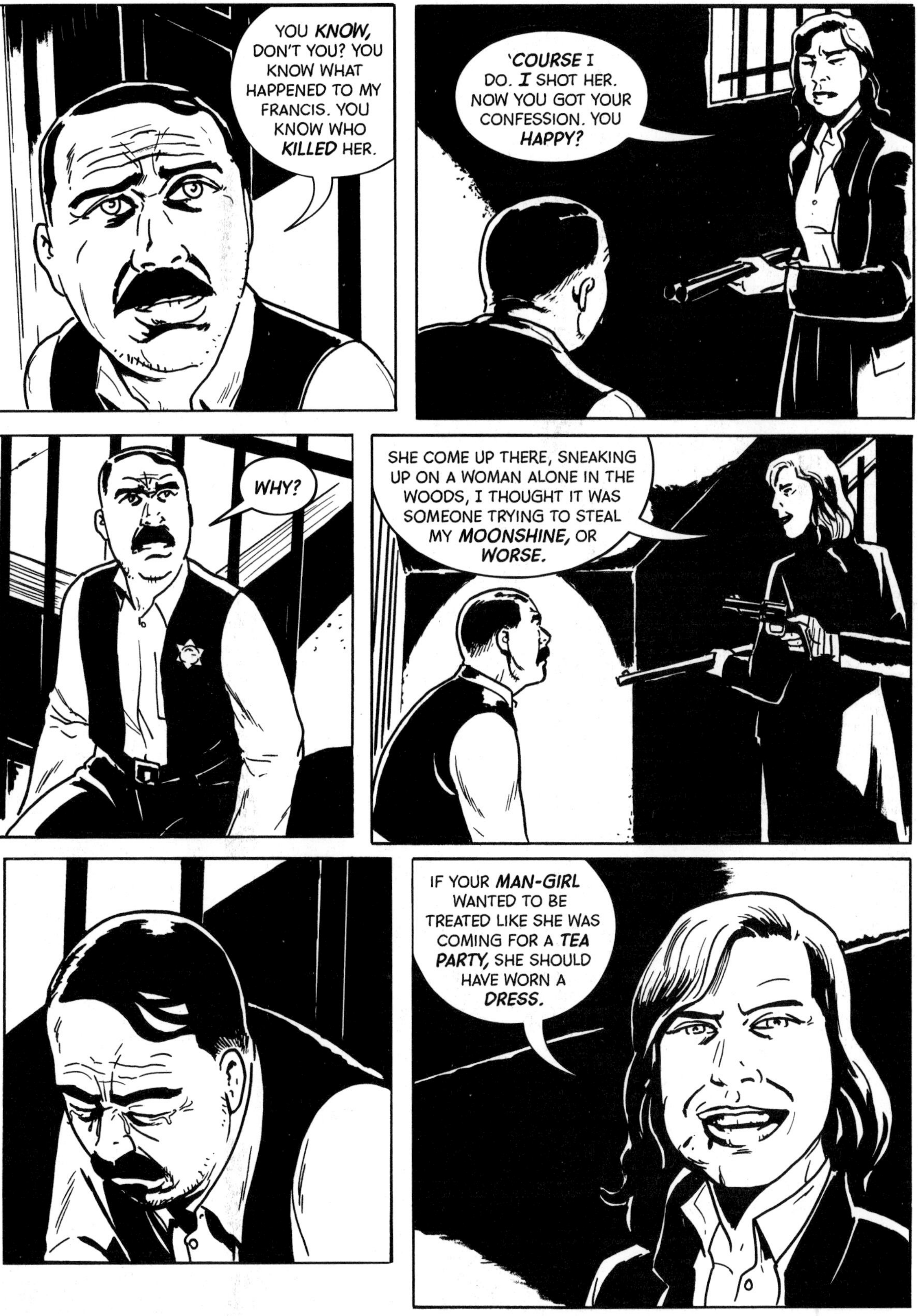
YOU KNOW, DON'T YOU? YOU KNOW WHAT HAPPENED TO MY FRANCIS. YOU KNOW WHO KILLED HER.
'COURSE I DO. I SHOT HER. NOW YOU GOT YOUR CONFESSION. YOU HAPPY?
WHY?
SHE COME UP THERE, SNEAKING UP ON A WOMAN ALONE IN THE WOODS, I THOUGHT IT WAS SOMEONE TRYING TO STEAL MY MOONSHINE, OR WORSE.
IF YOUR MAN-GIRL WANTED TO BE TREATED LIKE SHE WAS COMING FOR A TEA PARTY, SHE SHOULD HAVE WORN A DRESS.

THAT WORKS FOR ME. JUST TWO THINGS I'M GOING TO NEED BEFORE I GO. THAT IS *MY* MAN OUT THERE, THE ONE THOSE GHOULS *MURDERED*.

I WANT A LIST OF THE MAIN PEOPLE INVOLVED, FOR PUBLICATION, SENT TO MY OFFICE IN HARLEM BEFORE THE END OF THE WEEK.

AND I WANT MY FRIEND'S *BODY* RIGHT NOW, TO TAKE *BACK* WITH US.

BOY, DON'T YOU KNOW A GIFT HORSE WHEN YOU SEE IT? I'M DOING THE DECENT, HONORABLE, DOWNRIGHT *GENEROUS* THING BY LETTING YOU AND YOUR BOOTLEGGING BROTHER OUT OF HERE *ALIVE*.

IF EVER THERE WAS A TIME *NOT* TO ACT LIKE A *DUMB NIGGER,* THIS IS *IT.*

I MAY BE A *DUMB* NIGGER, BUT I'M NOT A *LAZY* ONE. I ALREADY WROTE AND FILED MY STORY WITH MY PAPER *TWO HOURS* AGO.

IT'S A SORDID TALE, ABOUT A CROSS-DRESSING CRACKER *DEPUTY,* AND THE ADULTEROUS *SHERIFF* WHO *DISCOVERED* HER.

NOW, IT HAS THE *SHERIFF* KILLING HER, AND *THAT* PART WILL NEED TO BE FIXED, BUT STILL, IF I DON'T SHOW UP IN HARLEM IN THE NEXT WEEK, MY EDITORS WILL *RUN* IT.

I'M *SYNDICATED,* DID I MENTION THAT? ON THE *BIG* STORIES, I'M EVEN IN THE *WHITE* PAPERS TOO.

WIRE SERVICE. MARVELS OF *MODERN MEDIA.*

OH YEAH, IF YOU COULD GET *PICTURES* OF ANYONE WHO WAS INVOLVED, THAT WOULD BE *GREAT.*

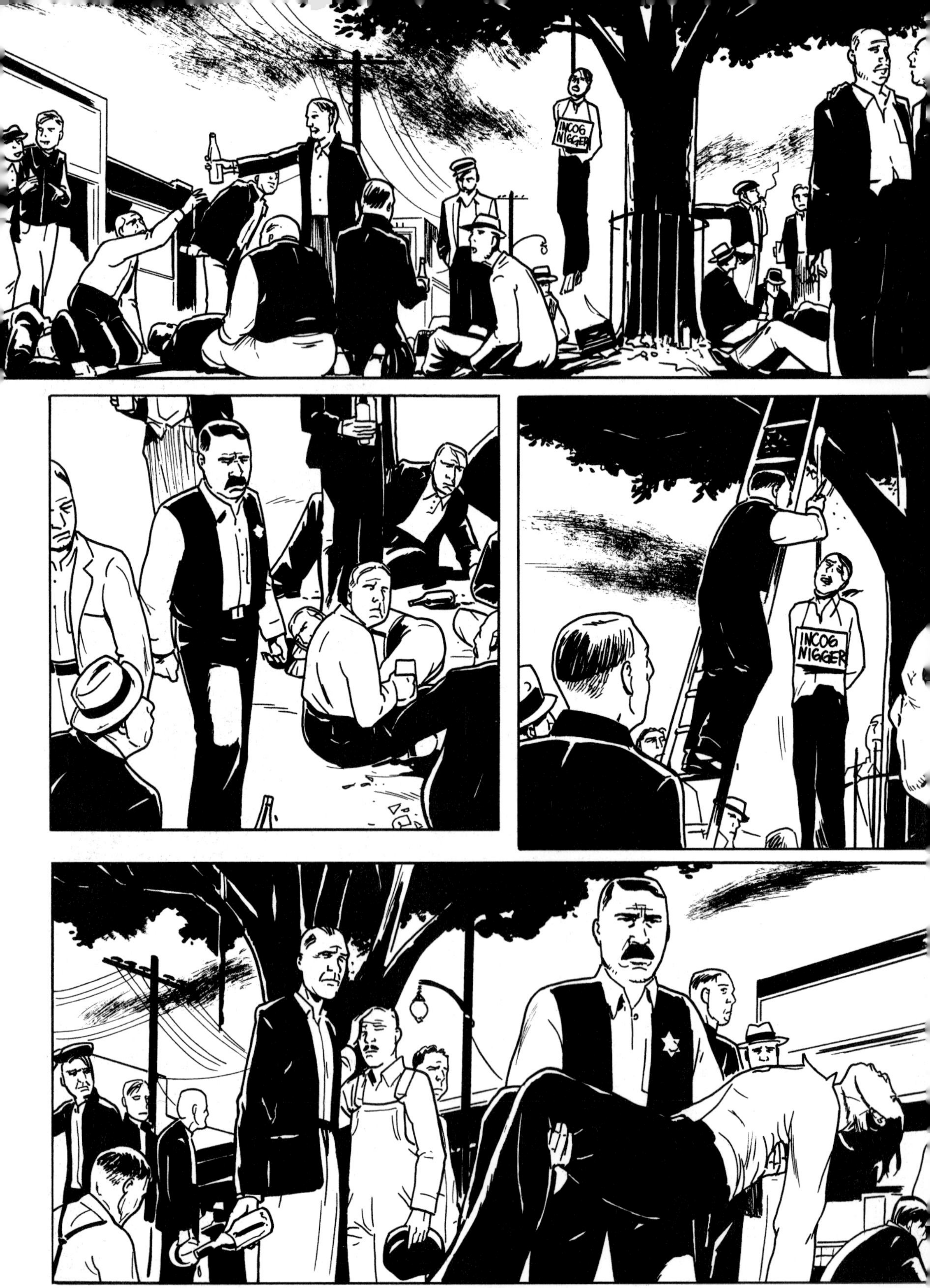
INCOG NIGGER
INCOG NIGGER

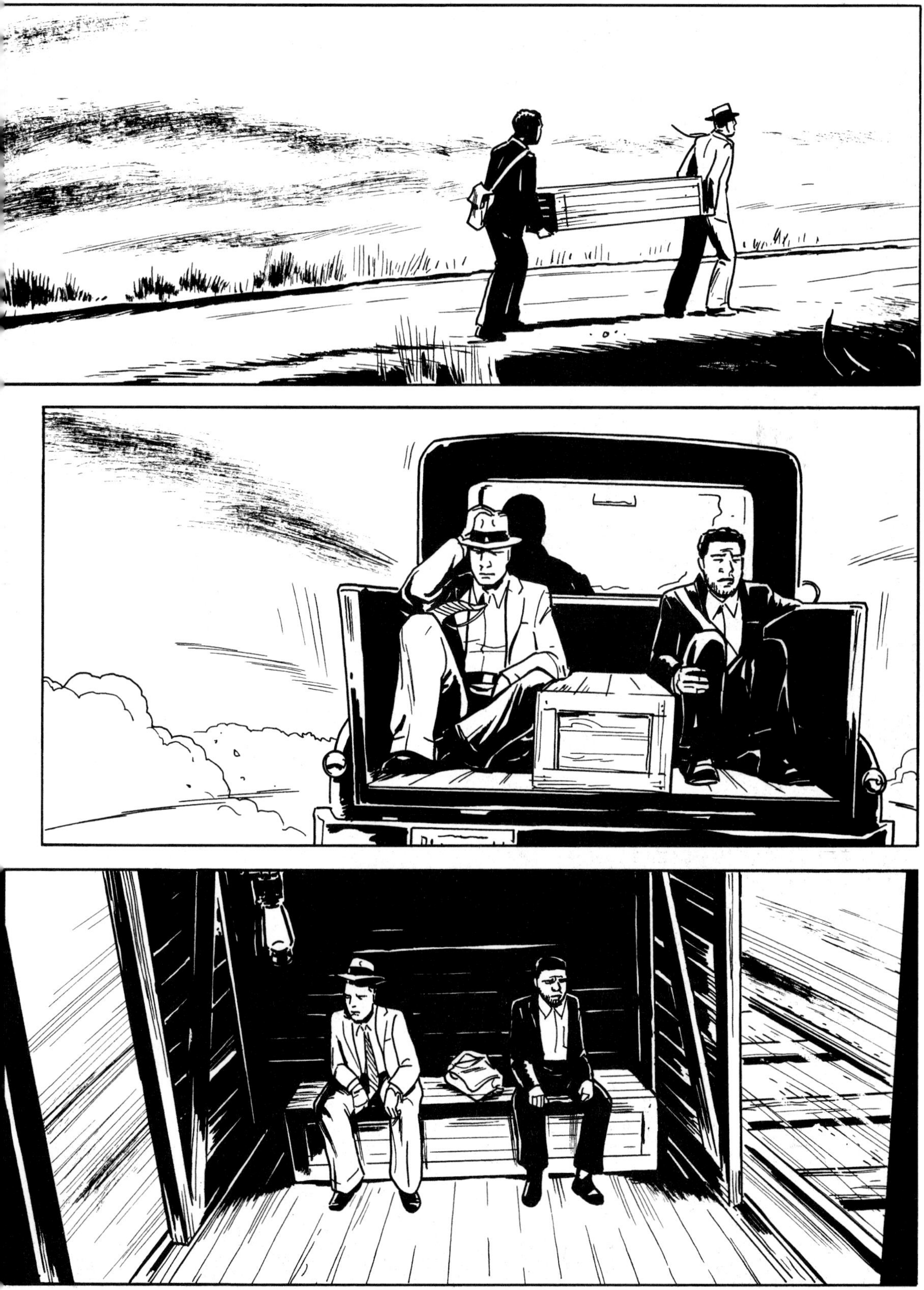

SO THIS IS IT. THIS IS HARLEM. IS IT LIKE YOU *THOUGHT* IT WOULD BE?

YUP. IT'S *JUST* LIKE I 'MAGINED. JUST AS BIG, JUST AS LOUD, JUST ABOUT THE SAME. I JUST NEVER IMAGINED *ME* IN A PLACE LIKE THIS.

WHAT THE HELL AM I GOING TO *DO* HERE?

WHAT CAN YOU DO? YOU CAN DO *ANYTHING*, PINCHY.

THIS IS THE LAND OF BLACK *LAWYERS*, BLACK *DOCTORS*, BLACK *BUSINESSMEN*. YOU CAN DO WHATEVER YOU *WANT* HERE. IT AIN'T LIKE THE *SOUTH*.

CAN I BREW MY *MOONSHINE* IN THEM *WOODS* THERE?

NO, PINCHY. THAT'S *CENTRAL PARK*.

I KNOW. THAT WAS A *JOKE*. BUT ME BEING *HERE* ISN'T.

YOU'RE RIGHT, IT'S *NOT* THE SOUTH. THIS ISN'T A *PLACE*, IT'S JUST A BUNCH OF *STRANGERS* PILING ON TOP OF EACH OTHER.

WE FROM THE SAME PLACE, THE SAME *WOMB* EVEN. IF I CAN ADJUST, SO CAN YOU. IT'S NOT *THAT* DIFFERENT. A LOT OF PEOPLE, BUT STILL THE SAME.

HERE, A *BLOCK'S* GOT ENOUGH PEOPLE FOR A *WHOLE TOWN,* AND IT *ACTS* LIKE THE SAME TOO.

YOU SHOP AT THE SAME CORNER STORE FOR A WHILE, YOU START TO SEE THE SAME FOLKS. YOU LEARN THEIR *STORIES,* THEIR *NAMES.* THEN IT DOESN'T *FEEL* SO BIG ANYMORE.

OKAY, FINE. IT'S JUST LIKE A SMALL TOWN. WHATEVER. BUT WHERE THE HELL DO *I* FIT IN? THIS PLACE AIN'T *FOR* THE LIKES OF ME. DON'T PRETEND DIFFERENT.

NO, YOU'RE RIGHT, THIS *ISN'T* A PLACE FOR A "BOOTLEGGING SCUMBAG."

BUT THIS IS NEW YORK. THIS IS HARLEM. THIS IS THE AGE OF THE *NEW NEGRO.*

HERE, THE POOR BECOME *RICH;* THE DESPISED, THE *ADMIRED.* YOU CAN *CREATE* ANY IDENTITY THAT YOU WANT.

SO *THAT'S* IT, I CAN JUST DECIDE TO BE A WHOLE NEW NEGRO? SO WHAT NEGRO *YOU* GOING TO BE, THEN?

THAT'S THE *BEST* THING: IDENTITY IS *OPEN-ENDED.* WHY HAVE JUST *ONE?*

SO, I BET NOW YOU ACTUALLY WANT ME TO GIVE YOU THAT *OFFICE* I PROMISED YOU?

HELL *YES* I DO.

AND I WANT THIS OFFICE NEXT TO *YOURS* TOO. SO I CAN *YELL* AT YOU THROUGH THE WALLS WHEN THE OCCASION ARISES.

GREAT. NOW I'M LOSING THE INCOGNEGRO COLUMN *AND* THE NEIGHBORHOOD'S GOING TO SHIT, ALL IN THE SAME DAY.

WRONG ON *BOTH* COUNTS. FIRST OF ALL, I WON'T *BE* HERE EVERY DAY.

NO. I WANT TO *KEEP* GOING INCOGNEGRO. SOMEBODY HAS TO. I CAN. SO I *WILL*.

BUT I WASN'T KIDDING ABOUT MY *ARTS* COLUMN. I'M DOING THAT *TOO*, AND I'M DOING IT IN *MY OWN NAME*.

I'LL JUST WEAR TWO *HATS*, SO TO SPEAK.

FINE. WEARING TWO HATS *SUITS* YOU.

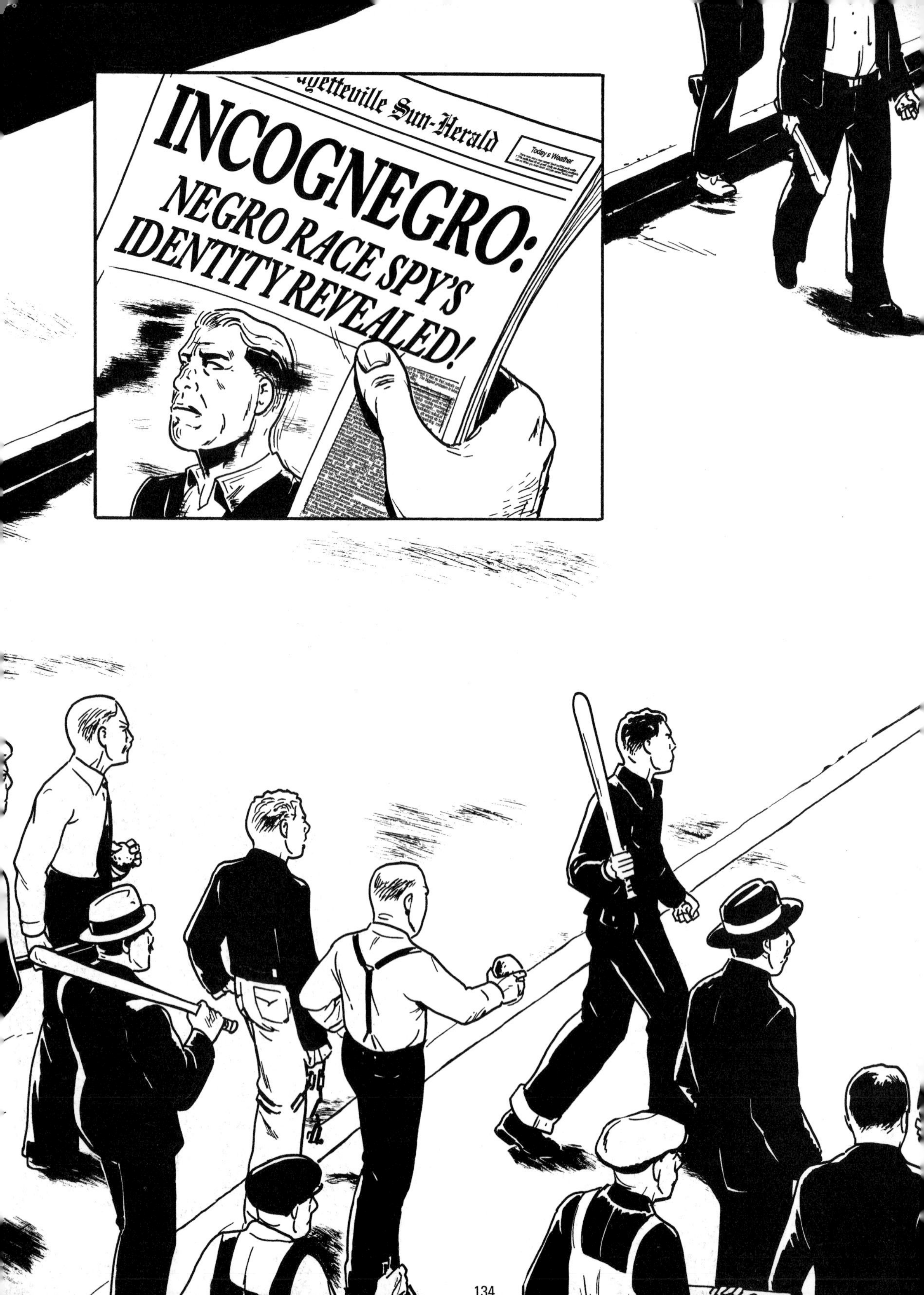
ayetteville Sun-Herald
Today's Weather
INCOGNEGRO:
NEGRO RACE SPY'S
IDENTITY REVEALED!

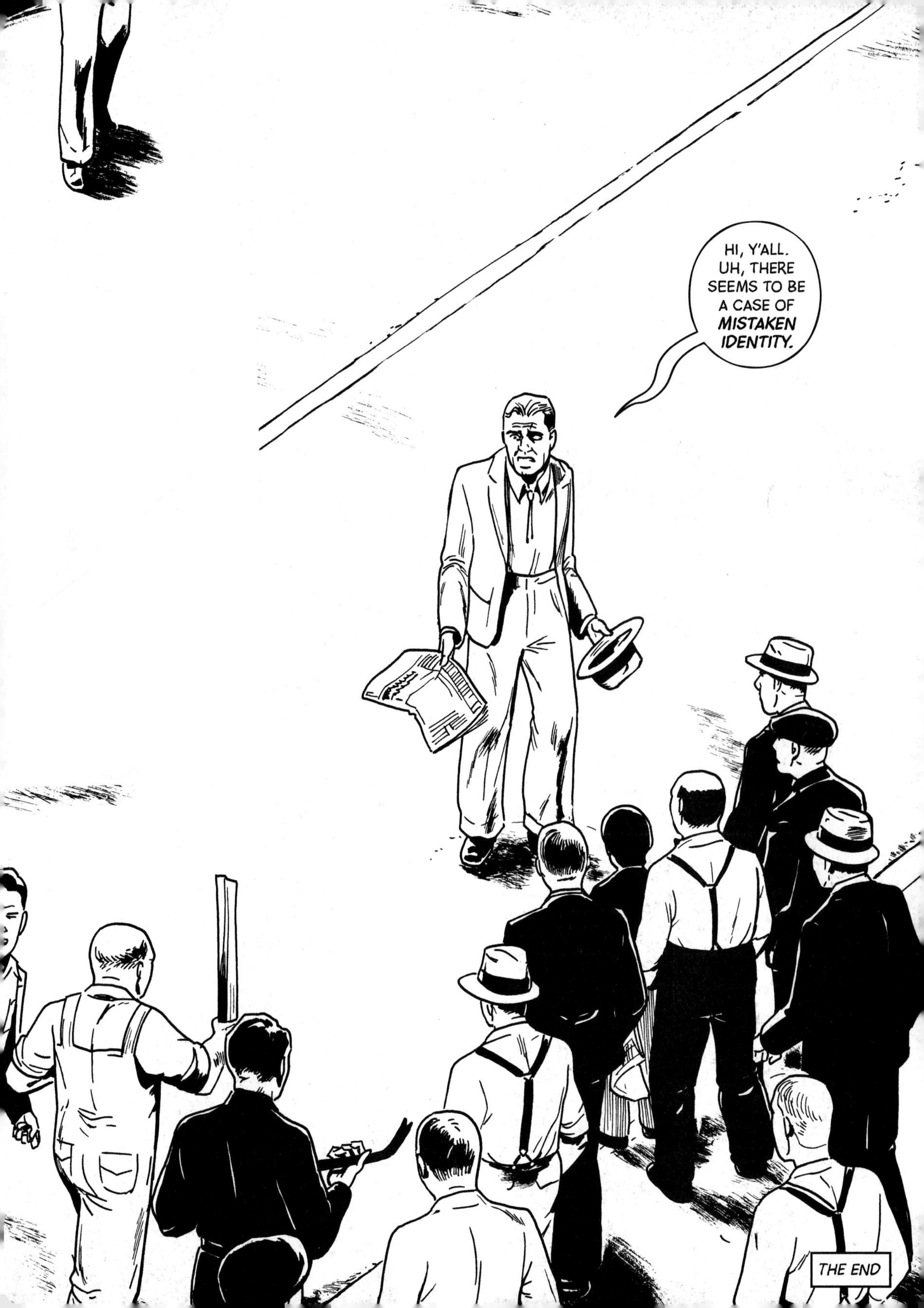
HI, Y'ALL. UH, THERE SEEMS TO BE A CASE OF *MISTAKEN IDENTITY.*
THE END

Mat Johnson is the award-winning author of the novels *Drop* and *Hunting in Harlem*, the nonfiction book *The Great Negro Plot*, and Vertigo's graphic novel *Hellblazer: Papa Midnite*. Mat is the recipient of the Hurston-Wright Legacy Award for fiction and the USA James Baldwin Fellowship for Literature. He is a writing professor at the University of Houston's Creative Writing Program and lives in the loop of Houston, Texas with his family.

Warren Pleece started drawing on his Dad's jazz records in the late '60s, before progressing through a greyish, '70s education to art college in the '80s. Inspired by old black & white films and fueled by the ridiculousness of Thatcher's Britain, he started the magazine *Velocity* with his brother, Gary, before moving on to work for Dark Horse and DC/Vertigo in the comics mainstream. He has worked on many titles for DC, including *True Faith*, *Hellblazer* and *Deadenders*, but still gets a kick out of drawing over priceless Blue Note album sleeves. He lives in Brighton, on the south coast of England, with his wife and two sons.